PRENTICE-HALL SERIES IN CURRICULUM AND TEACHING

Ronald T. Hyman, Consulting Editor

Differentiated Staffing—**Dempsey & Smith**
Designing Classroom Spontaneity: Case–Action Learning—**Nutting**
Discovery: A Challenge to Teachers—**Morine & Morine**
An Instructional Theory: A Beginning—**Hosford**
Instructional Implications of Inquiry—**Ryan & Ellis**
Discovering Your Teaching Self: Humanistic
Approaches to Effective Teaching—**Curwin & Fuhrmann**

Discovering Your Teaching Self

Humanistic Approaches to Effective Teaching

Richard L. Curwin
State University of New York at Geneseo

Barbara Schneider Fuhrmann
Virginia Commonwealth University

Prentice-Hall, Inc., Englewood Cliffs, New Jersey

Library of Congress Cataloging in Publication Data

CURWIN, RICHARD L. 1944–
  Discovering your teaching self.

  (Prentice-Hall series in curriculum and teaching)
  Bibliography: p.
  1. Teaching. I. Fuhrmann, Barbara Schneider,
1940– joint author. II. Title.
LB1025.2.C87   371.1'02   74-11371
ISBN 0-13-216085-4
ISBN 0-13-216077-3 (pbk.)

© 1975 by Prentice-Hall, Inc.
Englewood Cliffs, N.J.

10   9   8   7   6   5   4   3   2   1

*Prentice-Hall International, Inc., London
Prentice-Hall of Australia, Pty. Ltd., Sydney
Prentice-Hall of Canada, Ltd., Toronto
Prentice-Hall of India Private Limited, New Delhi
Prentice-Hall of Japan, Inc., Tokyo*

To
David J., David L., Andrew S., Geri, Bob, and Jeanette

Discovering Your Teaching Self

Contents

3 EXAMINING YOUR TEACHING SELF 105

Acknowledgments

This book grew out of our dissatisfaction with traditional teacher training and out of our interest in affective education and the implications it holds for positively affecting teacher education. For their invaluable assistance and support, we thank:

Sid Simon, who taught us the clarification process and the vital significance of values that underlies our work, and who gave us the basis for many of the book's activities. He provided us with the opportunity to develop at many levels, and gave us his love;

Gerry Weinstein, from whom we learned many processes of humanistic education, and who encouraged us to make it on our own;

Geri Curwin, whose creative energy invariably came alive when ours lagged;

Dwight Allen, who dared us to experiment and who supported our efforts;

Dick Clark, who gave us the freedom and opportunity to plan our own program;

The School of Education at the University of Massachusetts, which gave us the freedom and resources to carry out the experiment;

The University of Massachusetts' education students, and the in-service teachers who participated in the Cuyahoga County Instructional Supervision Study, who helped us refine and validate our work;

The schools of Amherst, Pelham, and Greenfield, Massachusetts, which allowed our students to work with their children;

All those people who responded to and encouraged our initial endeavor, especially Art Rittenberg and Ted Arnold of Prentice-Hall for their gentle support, and Ron Hyman of Rutgers University, for his belief in us and in our potential; and

Debbie Bond, who carefully prepared the final manuscript.

Barbara Fuhrmann
Richmond, Virginia

Rick Curwin
Geneseo, New York

Foreword

TEACHER SELF-KNOWLEDGE

We are in the midst of an expanding wave of educational activity commonly known as *humanistic education*. More books and instructional materials pertaining to this movement have appeared in the last two or three years than in all preceding years put together.[1] Teacher-training institutions around the nation have set up special departments for training specialists in humanistic education and have developed courses or workshops that are humanistically oriented.[2] "Humanizing education" is rapidly becoming an integral part of the schoolman's rhetoric. To prevent this rhetoric from remaining mere rhetoric, as so often happens with educational innovations, I would like to set forth my understanding of what humanistic education is all about and how it pertains in particular

[1] Canfield, John T. and Mark Phillips, "A Guide to Humanistic Education," *Paper Dragon #4*, Association for Humanistic Psychology, San Francisco, Calif. (undated).
[2] The Association for Humanistic Psychology keeps an up-to-date catalog of these activities.

to self-knowledge, to teaching, and to *Discovering Your Teaching Self: Humanistic Approaches to Effective Teaching.*

To say one is a humanistic educator sounds timely and ethically correct, but what does it really mean? I see this movement as an attempt to personalize education. It is part of a general societal reaction against the excesses of the scientific and technological norms and values that seem to have dehumanized the individual. We have been through an era in which the technical solution to problems reigned supreme and unquestioned. The technocrats, the efficiency experts, the scientists, all those who "can get *things* done," have been and still are our country's elite. This highly valued way of being by doing was reflected in the curriculum-reform movement in education that began in the fifties. The reform consisted of making the curriculum more structured, more cognitive, more scientific, more behaviorally objective, and above all, more efficient. It was thought that learning could now take place with a minimum of complications.

Then came the turbulent sixties with assassinations, racial strife, riots, and a continuing unpopular war, events that blatantly contradicted the promise of control over ourselves, our society, and the environment that our phenomenal technical achievements offered us. The credibility of the depersonalized technological elite has been eroded. "Instead, modern man [has begun the search] for 'identity,' for 'meaning,' for 'authenticity,' for 'soul,' for 'himself.' " [3] Educators interested in this search have begun to ask themselves some old questions with new strenuousness:

What is really learned in schools?

Are we teaching what we think we're teaching?

What is really worth teaching?

How can what's worth teaching be taught?

What really happens to the *person* behind the *role* in our educational process?

Who is the *person* who is the student?

Who can that person become?

Who is the *person* who is the teacher?

Who can that person become?

How can the basic human concerns for "Identity, Connectedness, and Power" [4] be met in our schools?

---

[3] Robert E. Magar, "Toward a Psychological Theory of Education," *Journal of Humanistic Psychology,* IX, No. 1, p. 14.
[4] Weinstein, Gerry and Mario Fantini, *Toward Humanistic Education: A Curriculum of Affect* (New York: Praeger, 1970).

A gradual proliferation of programs, methods, strategies, and tactics, all of which claimed to be "humanistic," arose in answer to such questions. How are we to know whether or not the claims are justified? I offer for consideration these criteria for evaluating such claims:

1. Does the program pay as much attention to personal knowledge (one's knowledge of oneself in relation to self, others, and society) as it does to public knowledge (knowledge of external realities)?

2. Is there a thorough integration of emotional, intellectual, and behavioral learning, with no one emphasized at the expense of the others?

3. Are the program goals and objectives congruent with the students' personal and professional needs?

4. Is the program geared more toward the liberation of the learner's unique life style than toward his domestication into preestablished norms and standards?

5. Does the program extend and expand the choices the individual has for responding to his world?

6. Does the program mutually enhance the growth of all of the participants? Is anyone's personal growth achieved at the expense of someone else?

In *Discovering Your Teaching Self: Humanistic Approaches to Effective Teaching* the authors offer a program of self-improvement for teachers and prospective teachers that grows out of these important humanistic criteria. Its emphasis on self-awareness and self-knowledge provides a vital framework for an exciting venture.

SELF-KNOWLEDGE

Self-knowledge has been part of western civilization's rhetoric for centuries: "Know thyself," "The unexamined life is not worth living," "To thine own self be true," "One cannot understand others without understanding one's self," "To know oneself is man's greatest achievement," and so forth. I use the term *rhetoric* very consciously, for while the above adages have been widely promulgated, their injunctions have rarely been infused into our educational institutions. Education has singularly devoted its energies to communicating knowledge about the world external to oneself—that is, "public knowledge,"—while completely ignoring knowledge of self, the internal or "personal knowledge" that one lives with most of the time.

Before I attempt to clarify the meaning of self-knowledge, it might be important to explore what self-knowledge is purported to achieve. According to Kubie, self-knowledge leads to greater creativity, a less distorted perception of reality, and greater freedom. "Just as the battle for political freedom must be won over and over again, so too in every life the battle for internal psychological freedom must be fought and won again and again, if men are to achieve and retain freedom from the tyranny of their own unconscious process, the freedom to understand the forces which determine their thoughts, feelings, purposes, goals, and behaviors. This freedom is the fifth and ultimate human freedom; like every other freedom, it demands external vigilance." [5] Karen Horney reinforces the connection between self-knowledge and freedom by maintaining that self-knowledge renders "a person free from inner bondages" and thus "make[s] him free for the development of his best potentialities." [6]

It has been Abraham Maslow's conviction that one of man's basic drives is the need to realize his potential, actualize himself, and grow. According to Goble, Maslow sees self-knowledge as a major means toward growth and actualization. "When a person understands himself he will understand his basic needs and true motivation and will learn to behave in a manner which will satisfy those needs. Self-understanding will also enable one to understand and relate to other people more effectively. If the entire human species has the same basic needs, then it follows that self-understanding leads to understanding of the entire human species." [7] To Harvey and Schroder, "it would appear axiomatic that he who knows himself best stands a better chance of controlling his environment and his own fate, in the sense of recognizing more clearly means-ends relationships and being able to reach a desired goal by alternate routes." [8]

It would seem, then, that knowing himself better ought to increase an individual's sense of control over his fate. By "sense of control" I mean the power to be intentional or more deliberate in one's response to life. Many of us proceed through life by employing whatever patterns of response we happen to find ourselves wearing. The same things continue to upset, please, anger, and frighten us. How often we hear the remark, "That's the way I am. I can't help myself, I've always been that way. It's my personality, part of my character structure, ever since I was a kid."

Self-knowledge increases the options for being, for going beyond un-

[5] Lawrence Kubie, "The Forgotten Man of Education," in *Contemporary Educational Psychology*, ed. Richard Jones (New York: Harper & Row, 1966), pp. 70–71.
[6] Karen Horney, *Self Analysis* (New York: W. W. Norton, 1942), pp. 21–22.
[7] Frank Goble, *The Third Force: The Psychology of Abraham Maslow* (New York: Grossman, 1970), p. 60.
[8] O. J. Harvey and H. M. Schroder, "Cognitive Aspects of Self and Motivation," in *Motivation and Social Interaction, Cognitive Determinants*, ed. O. J. Harvey (New York: Ronald Press, 1963), p. 129.

satisfying habitual responses. But what is self-knowledge, this potent wisdom that is supposed to lead one to greater freedom?

A comprehensive analysis of self-knowledge is beyond the scope of our requirements here; we need only a useful working definition of the predictive aspect of *self-knowledge*. First of all, when you know yourself you are essentially claiming to be predictable to yourself. The predictability of self-knowledge is exemplified in such statements as "Well, I know that I anger easily," or "I just can't stand children whispering while I'm talking," or "I get very nervous in the presence of an authority figure." These are all examples of predictable, anticipated modes of response to recurring stimuli. The only element missing from these examples that we include as part of our definition of self-knowledge is a description of the consequences that usually occur when the habitual response is made. Thus a complete working definition of this predictive aspect of self-knowledge would be "a verbal description of one's characteristic or habitual internal and external responses (thoughts, feelings, and actions) to a set of similar stimuli, and the consequences of those specified responses." Here is an example:

> I am threatened by authority figures. This occurs whenever I have to present something or be evaluated by someone who represents an authority to me. My internal responses are to have feelings of "butterflies" in my stomach, a lump in my throat, a quickening of my heart beat. My thoughts are, "he will think I'm stupid or I don't know how to do a good job." My external response is usually characterized by blushing and feeling my ears become red. My actions are to be prepared to the greatest possible degree so that I cannot fail to do a "good" job. In addition I try to avoid confrontation (even contact) with authority figures, thus avoiding feelings of discomfort. This means that I also miss many positive opportunities for interaction as well.[9]

Most of the activities in this book are intended to generate data, i.e., units of self-knowledge, regarding your personal responses to classroom stimuli. These activities will be catalytic insofar as you, the teacher, clarify aspects of your behavior that might have been taken for granted, or that you might have considered fixed and unalterable. But if, as I have already mentioned, the product of self-knowledge is to create more *response-ability,* more choice, then just being able to describe one's habitual pattern will not necessarily lead to more choice. Understanding, clarifying, and admitting to yourself the structure of your response pattern is a necessary but insufficient condition for creating alternative responses.

---

[9] G. Weinstein and Al Alschuler, Working Paper #3, *Autology,* unpublished (Amherst, University of Massachusetts, 1972).

There must also be a commitment to experiment with alternative responses. Awareness and insight are not enough. Knowing, as in the preceding example, that one feels intimidated by authority figures, or that one experiences a sense of incompetency, or that one "feels stupid," does not necessarily change those feelings. Knowing is a necessary step, however, for there are some people who would hesitate to disclose even to themselves that such feelings exist, and before we can experiment, we must know the reality of our personal situation in order to know what it is we are experimenting with.

In order to transform increased self-knowledge into an increased choice of responses, the following steps are suggested:

1. Having completed an activity in this book, ask yourself in what ways your response was typical of the way you respond to situations outside of class. What conditions must be present for you to respond that way?

2. Be sure you know as fully as possible what your response is. What are the feelings, judgments, and thoughts you have when you respond as you do? Unless you inventory your internal responses as well as your behavior, your self-knowledge will be limited.

3. Once you have clarified as elaborately as possible your response and the consistency with which you respond that way in similar situations, you are ready to ask: What does responding this way do for me? How does this pattern of response serve me? What does responding this way help me *get,* help me *avoid, protect* me from? In the preceding authority example the response protected the person from being evaluated, from being seen as incompetent or stupid, and finally, from facing his feelings about himself as incompetent or stupid.

4. Now we ask, If this is my typical response in these circumstances, and this is what the response does for me, *what price do I pay* for responding this way? Again, in our authority example the person mentioned his price: "This means that I also miss many positive situations for interactions as well."

5. Now we reach the experimentation phase. What are all of the different responses I might "try on"? It would be most helpful to complete the activities in this book in a small support group with two other teachers. (I have found three to be the ideal size for a support group working on self-knowledge.) Your group or you alone might now engage in a brainstorming session to see how many original and imaginative ways of response you can enumerate. These suggestions can be whimsical or sober, but the main idea is

quantity, not quality. From this list of possibilities you select one or two experiments that seem significant, achievable, and appropriate for you. As an illustration, the person in our authority example could have picked from a list of alternatives the following experiment: Whenever I confront an authority figure, I will say to myself, "No matter what you think, I am satisfied with my competency and intelligence. I am really a very competent and intelligent person!" The strategy here is to learn to affirm one's self more deliberately. It would also be very helpful if, after choosing an experimental strategy, you develop a contract with your support group in which you detail the steps you intend to pursue, the times when you will take these steps, and a time for reporting your progress to at least one other person.

6. Having "tried on" the alternative for a reasonable length of time, you can evaluate the consequences and determine whether or not there are any significant advantages in retaining the alternative as part of your repertoire. Hopefully you now have a choice, which is the major objective of self-knowledge.

The activities in this book will help you generate knowledge about your teaching self and appropriate personal alternatives. Welcome to the adventure, the humanistic adventure of creating knowledge and freedom for you, the *person* in the role of teacher.

Gerald Weinstein
Amherst, Massachusetts

Discovering Your Teaching Self

1

Discovering
Your Teaching Self

What I see is clearly affected by my values and prejudices and biases. I see bureaucratic waste and inefficiency; I see underdogs; I see dangerous reactionism, where other men might see a tight administrative ship, inferior social classes, and endurance of the good old ways. Sometimes I do not see anything intelligible because so much goes by so fast. At other times, I fail to see enough because I have only looked for things at which I had some prior intention to look. Often, my perceptual distortions arise from my tendencies to understand events as I have understood events previously. I fit new things into old patterns, even when the fits are poor. I frequently fuse inferences with perceptions and believe that I have seen things that are invisible, for example, that people like or don't like me. I even think I see invisible relationships, such as in cause-and-effect, and even more often I see "effects" for which I imagine erroneous causes. Whatever I see as figure, I have made figure. To have shifted my gaze thirty degrees would have generated different figures in different grounds.[1]

[1] Robert Goldhammer, *Clinical Supervision* (New York: Holt, Rinehart and Winston, 1969), p. 290.

RATIONALE

Discovering Your Teaching Self: Humanistic Approaches to Effective Teaching is a collection of activities that comprise a program for increasing your potential as a teacher. All people, including teachers, have untapped potentials; when these potentials are allowed expression, a tremendous personal growth is the result.

The activities in this book are divided into two sections. The first, "Awareness of Your Teaching Self," chapter two, deals with your awareness of yourself as a teacher—your ideals, beliefs, attitudes, values, and goals. The second, "Examining Your Teaching Self," chapter three, deals with the collection and interpretation of significant data about your teaching. The activities in "Awareness of Your Teaching Self" are internally focused; those in "Examining Your Teaching Self" are externally focused. Through the activities in chapter two we hope that you become aware of the teacher you are now and the teacher you would like to be. The activities in chapter three are designed to help you become the teacher you would like to be, to help you make your classroom behavior congruent with your ideals. *As your behavior becomes increasingly congruent with your ideals, you will be realizing your potential.*

The pre-service and in-service teachers with whom we have worked attest to our belief in the individual's ability to take responsibility for himself, and with some support and a commitment to self-growth, to realize his potential. *Discovering Your Teaching Self* is based on the assumption that you are responsible for being the teacher you want to be. The activities in this book will help you to ask useful questions and to find personally meaningful answers from your classroom, colleagues, students, and most importantly, from yourself. *But you alone are responsible for facilitating and realizing your own development.*

As you assume responsibility for your development as a teacher and become aware of your potential, you will be able to increase your response-ability to yourself and your environment, including your students and colleagues. You will increase your repertoire of possible responses and learn to respond uniquely and appropriately in every situation.

Note the behavior of the teacher in each of the following situations:

Mr. Jones, lecturing on molecules, notices John with his French book open. He walks to John's desk, slams the book shut, and tears up the paper John has been working on.

During standardized reading tests, Sally raises her hand. Mr. Arnold responds, "I told you there were no questions allowed!"

Because Miss Krantz has scheduled a fifteen-minute activity for the end of the class, she stops heated student discussion in order to complete her plans.

In each of the situations described above, a stimulus (the French book, the raised hand, the planned activity) produces a response on the part of the teacher, with varying degrees of conscious processing between the stimulus and the response in each case. At the simplest level a stimulus produces an immediate, reflexive response, with little or no thought occurring between the two. For example, a child learns quickly that a hot stove is painful and after only one experience automatically removes his hand from the heat of the burner. He does not consider other possible behavior, like turning off the stove, but simply reacts without a conscious consideration of alternative responses. This almost reflexive reaction can be viewed as in Fig. 1.1.

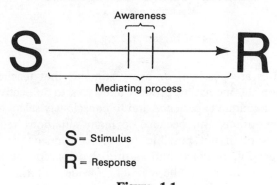

Figure 1.1

Between the overt stimulus of the hot stove (S) and the overt response of removing his hand (R), a mediating process occurs in which the individual's subjective activity (his awareness of the stimulus and the meaning he makes of it) determines his response. In the case of the hot stove, very little of this subjective mediating process is in the conscious awareness of the child, who reacts without conscious decision and in a highly limited manner. Given the circumstances, only one response is probable.

In the three teaching situations given above, the portion of the mediating process between S and R that is in awareness is expanded somewhat and the range of possible responses is increased. Mr. Jones could have requested that John read his French book later, he could have ignored his reading, or he could have suggested that John go to the library to work alone. Mr. Arnold could have responded to Sally in any number of ways, and Miss Krantz could have reevaluated her schedule in light of the students' discussion. With a greater portion of the mediating process brought into awareness, the number of possible responses is increased, as shown in Fig. 1.2.

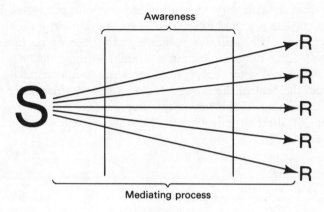

Figure 1.2

Many responses are possible for every stimulus that teachers face. In the ideal situation the mediating process allows us to subjectively analyze each stimulus as a unique experience and to consciously select the response that is most appropriate. But because so many situations require immediate action, it is often not possible (or recommended) to spend time analyzing each possible response and its probable consequences. When the child's hand is on the stove, he cannot consider alternatives without getting seriously burned. It is possible, however, to take time from our daily lives to consider alternative responses to the recurring stimuli in our teaching. We can thereby effectively increase our repertoire of possible responses, thus increasing our ability to act in unique and appropriate, rather than stereotyped, ways.

The mediating process between a stimulus (S) and a response (R), which is composed of our subjective reaction to the stimulus, the meaning we find in the stimulus, and our selection of a response to the stimulus, is influenced by various factors that effectively screen out some responses while making others more probable. Figure 1.3 presents the minimal basic factors—past experiences, feelings, values, beliefs and attitudes, perception of the teaching self, goals, aspirations, and outside influences

—that contribute to the screening processes in our daily responses to classroom situations.

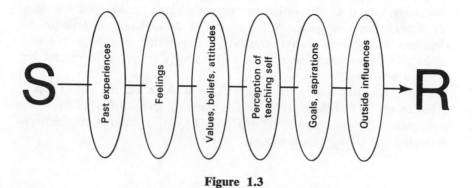

Figure 1.3

Given all possible responses, our *past experiences* lead us to prefer some possible responses and eliminate others. Mr. Arnold may have experienced numerous situations in which students failed to listen carefully; therefore he assumes that Sally has not listened. His past experiences limit his repertoire of responses to Sally's raised hand, as shown in Fig. 1.4, in which certain responses, indicated by dotted lines, are eliminated by being screened through Mr. Arnold's past experiences.

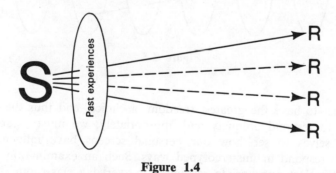

Figure 1.4

His *feelings* (both those related directly to the immediate situation and those that have resulted from outside experiences) also serve as a screen to some responses. If he is angry at the time Sally raises her hand, the possibility of his responding in an acceptant manner is decreased. The other factors operate similarly. If Mr. Jones *believes* that students will become responsible citizens by acquiescing to authority, he is unlikely to allow students to ignore his direction. If Miss Krantz *perceives herself* as competent only when she completes her scheduled plans, she is unlikely to stray far from them. If one of Mr. Jones's *goals* as a teacher is to have every student knowledgeable about molecular theory, his goal may have helped to determine his negative response to John's reading his French book. Finally, perhaps one of Miss Krantz's *favorite instructors* in education always stressed the importance of making realistic, achievable lesson plans, so that now she always strives to complete her planned activities.

Figure 1.5 graphically demonstrates how these factors of (1) past experiences, (2) feelings, (3) values, beliefs, and attitudes, (4) self-perceptions, (5) goals and ambitions, and (6) outside influences effectively determine our choice of a response.

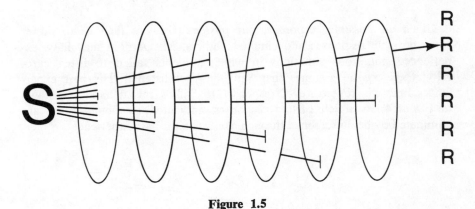

Figure 1.5

In order to have the greatest freedom of choice, and thus the greatest capacity to respond uniquely and appropriately, we must examine our teaching selves to see how our personal screens have influenced our ability to respond in unstereotyped ways. Such an examination will enable us to select appropriate responses to everyday classroom situations more effectively.

ILLUSTRATIONS

Here are two illustrations of teachers who have used the activities in this book to increase their response-ability.

Ken is a tenth-grade English teacher. From the time he began teaching, he felt that critical thinking was the most important learning that he could foster in his students. He spoke a great deal about how the students in his school never thought things out for themselves and usually depended on either authority figures or peers to make decisions for them. His goal was to develop critical thinking skills. However, little seemed to be happening in Ken's class discussions, in which he hoped to stimulate critical thinking. The students were passive, and Ken felt that he was forcing the answers out of them. So Ken decided that he would examine his questioning technique and see if he might discover something significant.

He used "What Kind of Questions Do You Ask?," which is included in chapter three. He analyzed the data and found that the majority of his questions were of the right-or-wrong variety. Realizing that critical thinking cannot be fostered by asking right-or-wrong type questions, he sought other alternatives. After considering many other types of questioning patterns, he resolved to change his behavior by asking at least fifty percent questions of opinion in his future class discussions. After a while he found that his discussions were more lively and interesting. Both he and his students seemed to be enjoying them more, and the level of thinking on the students' part seemed to be increasing. At the end of a month he did the activity over again to see if he had actually changed his behavior. The data showed that he was asking opinion questions seventy-five percent of the time. Ken had successfully changed his behavior to be congruent with one of his educational goals.

Ellen is a first-grade teacher who discovered that she wanted to come in close physical contact with her students after doing the activity "Real and Ideal Teacher," p. 20. She decided to see if she behaved in accordance with her ideal by using the activity "Teacher-Walking Map," p. 175. She found through an analysis of the data that she moved easily about the room and that she was close to all her students with the exception of three boys who usually sat together in the same corner of the room. Coincidentally, these same three boys were a concern for Ellen because they had shown little interest in the reading-readiness program that she had developed and was in the process of implementing. She determined that her avoidance of the boys was no coincidence, so she resolved to try a new behavior. She considered various alternatives: changing the boys' seats so that they did not sit together, spending as much time near the boys as she did with other students, and spending more time with them than with the rest of the class. She resolved to try to spend as much time near the boys as near other children without changing their seats. After trying her new behavior, she found that the boys' interest in the program had not increased, but she felt more comfortable in accepting their reluctance. By becoming aware of her avoidance and facing it, she was able to at least partially resolve an uncomfortable situation.

Both Ken and Ellen made their behavior more response-able and congruent with their beliefs. They proceeded through the following stages.

PROCESS FOR CHANGE

Stage One: Self-Awareness

Self-awareness refers to your understanding and awareness of the factors that screen your responses: past experiences, feelings, values, beliefs, attitudes, perceptions of your teaching self, goals, aspirations, and outside influences, as they relate to your teaching. Your screens provide you with direction and motivation for change.

Ken and Ellen both used self-awareness as a starting point. Ken's awareness of his goal of fostering critical thinking led him to discover that he was not accomplishing that goal. Ellen's awareness of her need to be physically close to her students was the basis for her subsequent actions. The activities in chapter two of this book are all aimed at increasing self-awareness.

Stage Two: Data Collection

You need data for comparing your ideals and your actions. The data must be nonevaluative and nonjudgmental. Ken used "What Kinds of Questions Do You Ask?," p. 199, to collect data; Ellen used the "Teacher-Walking Map," p. 175. The activities in chapter three are all designed for data-collecting.

Stage Three: Data Interpretation and Pattern Identification

Raw data reveals little about our teaching. It must be examined, with particular attention to pattern identification. Once the patterns are identified, you can begin to look at what the patterns mean in terms of effects and their congruence with your ideals. Ellen, for example, noticed that her pattern of avoidance was contradictory with her stated belief. Thus she was mobilized into new action.

Stage Four: Generating and Choosing Alternatives

Once you have looked at your data and discovered areas in which you wish to implement change, you need to generate alternative behaviors for experimentation. Ken, for example, considered possible changes he could make in his questioning pattern; Ellen thought of various alternatives that she might try with the three boys. Each then chose one alternative for experimentation. Notice that Ken and Ellen were specific in their descriptions of their alternatives. Choosing an alternative is an important step, and we believe that with experience and practice you can learn to be a better chooser.

Stage Five: Experimenting with the Alternative

Once you have chosen an alternative, it can be tested in a real-life situation. You can try the new behavior to see if it is comfortable for you and to see if the alternative meets your needs. Try the behavior long enough so that it is given a fair chance.

Stage Six: Adoption or Rejection of Alternatives

After trying the alternative, you are able to adopt it because it is congruent with your ideals and comfortable for you or to reject it as not beneficial for you. You may also decide to modify this new behavior to better fit your personality and ideals.

Stage Seven: Recycling

Growth involves change. A behavior is not permanently adopted, modified, or rejected. Further input and new perspectives bring different considerations, so a decision may be changed or reconsidered any number of times. To take into account these changes, you can begin stage one over again and repeat the cycle.

CONCEPTS THAT AID CHANGE

It is helpful for you to understand several of the concepts behind the process of change.

Self-contracts. Self-contracts are resolutions that *you write for yourself* to try new behavior. When Ken resolved to ask opinion questions, he wrote a self-contract that stipulated what his new behavior would be. Self-contracts are more useful if they are specific—it is better to resolve to ask fifty percent more opinion questions, as Ken did, than it is to resolve to be a better questioner. Self-contracts can be very personal; therefore you always have the right of privacy. You should never share a self-contract unless you choose to do so; likewise, you should never in-sist that someone else show you his self-contract.

In pre-service courses based on the activities in this book, we asked each student to write a self-contract per week and to hand them in even-tually with an analysis of how well each contract was fulfilled. The con-tracts were kept in envelopes with the students' names (they were not read by us) and at the end of the semester they were returned to the students who wrote them. It was of great interest for the students to look back over the semester and see what resolutions they made and how well they were followed.

Learning partners or observers. In many of the activities in the data-

collection section of the book you are asked to use an observer to gather information about your teaching. Your observer will come into your room and watch you teach different lessons at different times. Ken's part-ner recorded his questions and Ellen's observer drew her teacher-walking map. It is very important to choose a partner you trust or with whom you can build a trusting relationship. Trust provides a climate for you to act openly and naturally with your observer in your room. To be ob-served is of little use if you act in a way that is not natural, for the data that your observer collects will not apply to your normal teaching.

Your learning partner and you should both understand that the data that is most helpful is *nonevaluative.* Leave all value judgments out of the collecting process. For example, it is evaluative to say, "You asked too many short-answer questions." This statement is a judgment that fails to account for the teacher's goal in the class. A better way to say it is "You asked fifteen short-answer questions out of twenty." Note the evaluation of Socrates on p. 11 in which the perspective of the evaluator very obviously influenced the evaluation.

TEACHER EVALUATION*

Teacher: Socrates

Comments

Rating (high to low)

	1	2	3	4	5	A. Personal Qualifications	Comments
1. personal appearance					x		Dresses in an old sheet draped about body
2. self-confidence					x		Not sure of himself—always asking questions
3. use of English			x				Speaks with a heavy Greek accent
4. adaptability					x		Prone to suicide by poison when under duress
						B. Class Management	
1. organization					x		Does not keep a seating chart
2. room appearance			x				Does not have eye-catching bulletin boards
3. utilization of supplies	x						Does not use supplies
						C. Teacher-Pupil Relationships	
1. tact and consideration					x		Places student in embarrassing situation by asking questions
2. attitude of class		x					Class is friendly
						D. Techniques of Teaching	
1. daily preparation					x		Does not keep daily lesson plans
2. attention to course of study		x					Quite flexible—allows students to wander to different topics
3. knowledge of subject matter					x		Does not know material—has to question pupils to gain knowledge
						E. Professional Attitude	
1. professional ethics					x		Does not belong to professional association
2. in-service training					x		Complete failure—not even attended college
3. parent relationships					x		Needs to improve—parents are trying to get rid of him

RECOMMENDATION: DOES NOT HAVE A PLACE IN EDUCATION—SHOULD NOT BE REHIRED

*John Gauss, *Phi Delta Kappan,* January 1962.

11

Examine the data your observer has collected as soon after teaching your lesson as possible. All data should be written, audio-taped, or video-taped—never rely on memory. Receive the information openly and nondefensively. As your trust level increases, your ability to be open and nondefensive will increase accordingly. Remember that if the data is free from value judgments, it can have no reflection on your teaching until you make meaning out of it. Once the data is clear to you, begin to make meaning out of it in terms of your interests, needs, and concerns. You may, of course, find it helpful to do this with the aid of your partner, but this means that you have included your partner in stage two and stage three of the change process. It is important to keep the two stages separate, and if your partner is going to work with you in stage three, keep the two functions separate. However you involve your partner, draw your own conclusions about your teaching. Test your conclusions with your partner, but do not substitute his conclusions for yours. You, and only you, are responsible for your actions, so you must act out of your desire for change.

The choice of your learning partner is an important one. Try to select a person who can be facilitative rather than authoritarian. If you are currently teaching, you might select a teacher from the same school and observe each other in a reciprocal arrangement. If you use a supervisor, work out the ground rules of trust, nonevaluative feedback, and facilitative dialogue before any actual observation takes place. Your observer is an aid to your growth, not a judge of your teaching.

Support groups. Many of the activities in this book, especially those in chapter two, can be used in group situations. We encourage you to

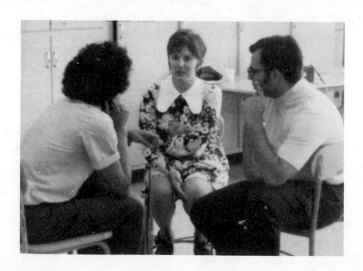

use groups whenever possible, for the creative energy and insights that come from group experiences cannot be matched by working alone. Moreover, the support and encouragement of a group will help you to experiment and make changes when the going becomes difficult. An ideal support-group size is between three and six members, though you may wish to combine small groups for activities that require more people. Like learning partners, groups must be built on trust, support, openness, and nondefensiveness.

If you are in a pre-service program, a natural support group can be formed with fellow students either as part of a class or on your own. A good source of support for student teachers are the other student teachers in your school. In-service teachers can form support groups with friends and colleagues on their staff. You might encourage your administration to form more formal support groups with scheduled meetings during released time or free periods, or you might find it helpful to form a support group with members from outside the school you are teaching in. Teachers from other schools, friends, and professional educators in the community are excellent candiates for membership.

Use your support group to develop interpersonal-relationship skills, communication skills, and as a source of feedback and input for discovering your teaching self.

Journals.   We encourage you to keep a record of your progress as you move in new directions by keeping a personal journal. We refer to journal entries in many of the activities in this book. Reflection is of great benefit, especially as you consider new directions for yourself, and we do not trust memory to provide food for that reflection.

You might include in your journal all the data collected by you and your partner, the insights gained from your support groups, all of your self-contracts with notes as to how each one is going, and any feelings, problems, puzzlements, or questions you have from your teaching or pre-service program. Ken, for example, recorded his frustration with his class discussions. When he noticed how often it appeared, he was able to consider why he felt so frustrated and to begin changing his related behavior.

Your journals are private and should be shared only with your consent.

Role-playing.   Role-playing is an imaginative series of enactments and reenactments in which you have the opportunity to analyze a problem, explore your feelings about it, and then consider many different alternatives and the consequences of those alternatives. We suggest in various activities that you role-play situations so that you can experience them in an environment that is safer than real-life situations. Other activities can be easily adapted for role-playing. As your support group begins to develop and grow, you can use role-playing to enact a wide variety of school situations for the group's input.

We have used role-playing to simulate classroom situations with both pre-service and in-service teachers. One teacher role-plays the teacher before the remainder of the group, who role-play students. For example,

one pre-service teacher role-played a situation with third-grade students. The teacher prepared a ten-minute lesson and received feedback from her pre-service peers, who used the activities in this book as a framework. You can also use role-playing techniques to generate feedback on how the group sees two learning partners giving and receiving nonevaluative feedback. Your support group is a natural place for this type of role-playing.

Brainstorming.   Brainstorming is a creative process in which ideas are generated openly and freely. As a regular feature of your classroom and support-group activity, brainstorming can provide for the development and expression of ideas in a supportive, energetic atmosphere. Brainstorming encourages half-formed ideas to grow collaboratively into real possibilities.

Brainstorming is a group activity that encourages acceptance and community support. Competition and failure are antithetical to brainstorming.

In a brainstorming session a problem is presented to the entire group. All solutions, however zany, unrealistic, or half-formed, are invited and accepted. Group members offer ideas as rapidly as they can while a few recorders write down every response on a chalkboard or on a large piece of newsprint (newsprint allows you to keep the responses). The freewheeling acceptant atmosphere allows members of the group to expand on one another's ideas, to "piggyback" ideas. The following *Rules of Brainstorming* should be posted and strictly adhered to:

1. Quantity counts.
2. Express every idea you have, regardless of how zany it may seem.
3. Make no judgments (do not vocally comment on the worth of ideas with "Good," "Good idea," "What's that mean?," etc.).
4. Try for far-out ideas.
5. Record every idea.

Following these simple rules will insure an atmosphere of acceptance and will encourage creative thought and interplay. The longer the list of ideas, the more likely it is to contain some truly useful and creative ones. Encouraging far-out ideas and forbidding judgments provides total acceptance and thus allows the expression of certain ideas and half-formed thoughts that in other more threatening situations might never surface. These might then be expanded on by others or might trigger another idea in another individual's thoughts. A totally new and highly creative idea often results from such interplay.

Brainstorming is a skill, so it can be improved with practice. To practice it with your class, you might use problems that seem far-out or silly, thus establishing a playful atmosphere in which far-out ideas are encouraged. For example, you might have the group brainstorm—

uses for a rubber band in an empty room;

ways to use six bricks;

ways to improve bicycles;

the selection of new art supplies for classrooms;

uses for paper clips.

In each instance stop the brainstorming session before ideas run out, thereby maintaining the excitement generated by the brainstorming itself. Once your students and colleagues learn the rules of brainstorming and have practiced it a few times, you will probably find brainstorming a useful way to generate ideas and solutions to all kinds of problems that arise, from how to manage the noise level in the classroom to how to devise better controls over neighborhood pollution problems.

ACTIVITY FORMAT

Most of the activities, with the exception of log conversations and a few simple, uninvolved experiences for which an extensive, standard format is inappropriate ("The Faculty Room," "School of the Future," "Teacher-

Education Program," "Schoolbag," "Bulletin Boards," "Time Analysis," "Open-ended Student Feedback"), are designed as follows:

Introductory paragraph

Objectives: Statements of purpose for activity

Directions: (Includes alternative methods)

Questions: Open-ended, nonevaluative means of self-assessment

Follow-up: Ways to implement new learning

Student Use: Ways to adapt the activity for use in classrooms with students of all ages. Both specific suggestions and more general ideas for modification are presented. (Not all activities include this section. In some cases the activity is designed solely to examine teacher behavior, and therefore a student application is inappropriate. In other cases we simply have been unable to modify the activity for students in a meaningful way. This does not mean, of course, that the activity cannot be modified for use with students. We invite you to create your own modifications and to share your ideas and experiences with us.)

LOG CONVERSATIONS

Early in the nineteenth century a remarkable man by the name of Mark Hopkins (president of Williams College) quite personally and in-

dependently influenced the process of higher education in America. He believed that it is a teacher's responsibility not merely to transmit knowledge from one source to another (books as well as people can do that), but to stimulate young minds to search for meaning. Mark Hopkins introduced the discussion method and was soon known for his powers of questioning and the lively exchange of views that occurred in his classes, both of which traits were immortalized by President Garfield in his description of a well-endowed college as "a log with a student on one end and Mark Hopkins on the other." [2]

We are frustrated because we cannot exchange views with our readers. We want to dialogue with you. Obviously the printed page, time, and distance stand in our way, so we have devised the closest substitute we can to an exchange with you. We have scattered throughout *Discovering Your Teaching Self* a number of quotations that raise important issues. Though the issues probably have no all-time "right" answers, we have indicated our feelings, attitudes, and thoughts on them, and we invite you to respond. Our responses are honest and real; we hope yours will be too. At the risk of presumption, we dare to call our personal dialogues with you *log conversations* as we and you temporarily occupy the log that Mark Hopkins made famous.

[2] John S. Brubacher and Willis Rudy, *Higher Education in Transition* (New York: Harper & Row, 1958), p. 86.

2

Awareness of
Your Teaching Self

Attitudes, feelings, goals, values, beliefs, and past experiences influence behavior. When I feel good about myself and my situation, I act in a manner that reflects my positive attitude; conversely, when I feel cynical or depressed or just tired, that attitude is reflected in my behavior. Everything I do, whether it's the way I walk or the way I respond to a student's glance, is intimately related to how I see myself and my environment and to how aware I am of the important influences on my behavior.

The activities in this chapter are designed to help you take a careful look at your attitudes, feelings, beliefs, and past experiences, especially as they relate to your teaching self. We offer you an opportunity to become aware of yourself and to relate your internal states to your behavior. At times you may find a conflict between your past actions and one of your beliefs. Such a discovery will probably make you uncomfortable because you will be living with dissonance. What you do about that dissonance, however, is up to you. You can ignore it, rationalize it, or project it onto others. You can also use it creatively by recognizing it, accepting it as an area of your life that needs attention, and adopting a plan of action to bring your behavior and beliefs into a greater congruence.

You will note that most of the activities in this chapter can be done alone, with a friend, or in a support group, whichever is most appropriate for you. Other activities require that you interact with people, but always remember that you have the right of privacy. Therefore you may pass at any time when working in a group.

These activities are intended to be personally involving. Take your time with them, use them meaningfully, and enjoy them.

REAL AND IDEAL TEACHER

Teaching often seems mysterious—part science, part art, and part magic. There are as many definitions of good teaching as there are books on the shelves of an educator's library. Many approaches to teacher improvement are like recipes that transform the teacher into cook, the materials into ingredients, and out comes "learning stew." This recipe approach ignores the distinct personalities of the teacher and the students. It overlooks the gestalt, or whole, of the classroom dynamics and particular situations. Its view of teaching is fragmented and unrelated to those involved in the learning cycle.

On the other hand, global approaches to teacher improvement can also be inadequate. Being very general, global approaches often have no real application for teachers. For example, a generality such as "A good teacher is friendly" tells us very little about our behavior, nor does it offer any directions for us to consider. Any approach that is going to improve teachers has to be specific and applicable.

"Real and Ideal Teacher" provides a third approach. You begin to identify areas of your teaching that you feel are in need of improvement and begin to set some goals for yourself as a teacher. You select the specific areas you wish to concentrate on at any one time.

Objectives

1. To express a metaphorical model of ideal teaching.
2. To express a metaphorical model of current teaching.
3. To identify ways to move toward your ideal.

Directions

Step One: Using a large sheet of art paper or newsprint and felt pencils or crayons, draw a picture of your ideal teacher. While the artwork of the picture is not important, carefully consider the elements that will be included. Use words only if they would normally be visible in the scene you have selected to depict. If you are working in a small group, you may wish either to draw individual pictures and compare or to draw a composite with each group member contributing part of the artwork. If you choose the latter method, discuss and reach consensus on each part of the drawing.

Once the drawing is finished, list the characteristics that apply to your creation. Many of these characteristics will already be evident in the design of the drawing, while other characteristics will be implied. If you are working in a group situation with more than one drawing, display each work and have a question-and-answer period, with the emphasis on sharing ideas.

Step Two: Draw a picture of how you currently picture yourself as a teacher. You may be as metaphorical as you wish, remembering again that the art work is only secondary to the process of self-discovery and self-examination. Use the procedures described in step one.

Step Three: When the two pictures have been completed and examined, lay them down and take a sheet of paper and place it between the two completed drawings. Consider what steps you might take in moving from the drawing of your current teaching self to that of your ideal. On this middle sheet of paper list as many steps as possible. Try to decide which steps come first, which are long-term, and which short-term. On a separate sheet draw a map that leads you from the current to the ideal. Place the shorter, more immediate steps closer to the current and the longer range goals closer to the ideal. You might use the model of a road map, a treasure map, or any other format that seems appropriate.

Questions

1. Which drawing was the more difficult to do? Why?
2. Which steps along your map do you feel the most confident of accomplishing? Which are you the least confident about?
3. Identify different resources—people, books, experiences—that will be useful in accomplishing your steps.

Follow-up

Keep a record in your journal of how you are actually moving on your map. Record in your journal each time you actually perform one of your steps and date it. List under the entry any circumstances that later will help you to recall the event in detail. Also list any unsuccessful steps that you tried, and attempt to identify how and why they failed. If you become aware that a step was unrealistic, eliminate it from your map and add a more realistic step. At the end of a month review your journal and note how well you are doing in quest of your ideal. Make all appropriate evaluative notations and any notes to yourself about future directions in your journal.

Student Use

This activity is readily adaptable for use with students of any age. You might choose an area for the class to work on, or you might let the class choose an area, or perhaps each student can work on an individual area. Although the latter method is the most preferable because it takes individual characteristics into account, any method can be extremely effective. Appropriate areas for students include athletics, school, peer relationships, family life, and outside hobbies. Using the example of peer relationships, junior-high students might each draw a picture of the ideal friend, employing the methods described in the first part of this activity. Each would then draw a picture of himself as a friend and would finally construct a map between the two drawings.

Remember that the ideal and current drawings must come from the perceptions of the student. Try not to influence the drawings by suggesting characteristics that you consider important.

LOG CONVERSATION: LEARNING IS NOT LIKING

Rick: Barbara, I saw this editorial in the paper last night. At first I couldn't decide whether the guy was facetious or for real. What do you think?

> In a conversation with a boy from Pittsburgh who wants to be an electrician and who likes mathematics, Mr. Nixon advised him to study "things you don't like" as well as subjects that interest him.
>
> The point was well taken, for there's a growing notion these days that liking and learning run together. They don't, or at least not necessarily.
>
> We all of us know young people who maybe dropped courses or didn't do well in them simply because they either didn't like the subjects or the teachers, or maybe both.
>
> But whenever was learning a likeable affair? When it happens that way, it's wonderful, but rare is the student who is well molded by enjoyable experience alone.
>
> I can think back, and so can you, to a couple of teachers much disliked at the time because we thought they were crabby or because they

gave us too much homework. But now, 30 or 40 years later, they look better and better.

I can remember, and so can all servicemen, detesting the rigidity and the regimentation of service life—and how about that drill instructor who made us squirm like worms! But in retrospect, the discipline wasn't all bad.

I can recall, and so can many people, plugging away at the pianoforte when I'd much rather have been playing football or soccer. But now, when I couldn't any longer play football or soccer even if I wanted to, I begin to realize that the forced apprenticeship had its blessings too.

I can also recall hating Latin, and so can you, and yet the mental discipline was useful.

A little compulsion in those early formative years, some knuckling down to disagreeable tasks, is part of growing up. And if that includes some learning by rote, so be it—where would we ever be without the little rhyme that goes, "Thirty days hath September, April, June and November . . ."

One of my favorite authors, the late Andre Maurois, once said this about the art of teaching and learning:

". . . There can be no teaching without discipline. A pupil must first learn to work.

". . . Training of the will must precede that of the mind, and this is why home teaching is never very successful. Excuses are too easily accepted: The child has a headache, he has slept badly, there is a party somewhere.

". . . To amuse is not to teach. The object of teaching is to erect a framework of knowledge in a child's mind and gradually to bring the child as near as may be to the average level of intelligence.

". . . That which is learned without difficulty is soon forgotten, and, for the same reason, oral instruction which does not require the pupil's personal participation is almost always rather useless. Eloquence slides in and out of young minds. To listen is not to work."

The difficult trick, I suppose, is to bend the mind early to the disliked as well as the liked, and then to hope that the effluxion of time, like the slow drawing back of a well-aimed bow, will launch us into careers that make it a pleasure to go daily to work.[1]

Barbara: I wish he were being facetious, but I doubt he is. I resent his assuming that he speaks for me when he says "and so can you" repeatedly. I remember some teachers I didn't (and still don't) like, but all I remember about them are the qualities that made me dislike them. I doubt that they taught me much. I just wasn't in a receptive mood around

---

[1] Des Stone, *Sunday Democrat and Chronicle* (Rochester, New York), December 2, 1972, Editorial page.

them. But I'm speaking only for myself. Do you readers recall any teachers you disliked but from whom you learned something significant?

You:

Rick: That statement about mental discipline being useful bothers me. I think today's modern math processes are more meaningful than our old way of memorizing without understanding. I always hated math, and now I still have trouble balancing my checkbook. I wonder what he means by "mental discipline." What do you readers think he means? Is it necessary? How does the "mental discipline" imposed by a hated subject serve you now?

You:

Rick: I think the author was justifying some very unpleasant school experiences. I wonder if he remembers what it was like to be miserable as a student.

Barbara: I've always hated math and I have trouble balancing my checkbook too. It also seems to me that the author has forgotten what it felt like to be a student. He is looking back, but he isn't reliving his experiences. For me, getting in touch with the reality of student life helps me judge what I now do and believe as a teacher. I'd now like to invite you, our readers, to experience your student days in the next activity, "There and Then."

THERE AND THEN

Effective, helpful teachers are able to understand and to empathize with their students. Each of us was at one time the age our students are now; each of us has a wealth of personal data to draw upon when we wish to examine the attitudes, thoughts, concerns, and feelings of our students. It is therefore useful for each of us periodically to step back in time to reexamine our days in school and recall the significant concerns we had as students.

Objectives

1. To recall the most significant concerns you had as a student at the age of your current students.
2. To become more sensitive to the concerns of your students.

Directions

Think back and recreate in your imagination an ordinary day at the time you were the age of your current students. Picture yourself in school, surrounded by the people and things that comprised your world at that time of your life. You may find it helpful to write your signature as you wrote it then. Focus on the things that were most important to you. If you teach young children now, try to recall your early elementary years. Get in touch with your childhood again. If you teach older children, remember what it was like when you were their age.

Then, in each of the four quadrants of the circle on the accompanying worksheet, write a word or a short phrase about something important you recall from those days. Each quadrant should represent a separate concern.

When you have identified four of your concerns at the age of your students, write a paragraph beginning "School for me was . . ," including an explanation of each of the concerns indicated in your "There and Then."

Questions

1. What kinds of concerns do you recall most readily? Are they concerned with subject matter? with learning? with attitudes and feelings? with peers? with social life?
2. What patterns do you see in your responses?

Follow-up

To help determine how well you understand your students, use a four-quadrant circle and fill it in as you think your students would if they were to do a "Here and Now" in which current rather than past concerns are identified. You can either do a collective "Here and Now" to represent a composite of the concerns of your class, or you might choose a few individual students and do a separate one for each of them. You can make your choices especially meaningful by choosing your most enigmatic students or by choosing a few students who are very different from each other. Do a "Here and Now" as you imagine each would respond.

Name: [As you would have written it]

_____

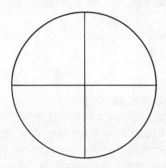

School for me was —

SEX, DRUGS, &

ROCK - N - ROLL !!!

To check your perceptions, introduce your students to the idea of a "Here and Now" as a means of helping us get in touch with what is going on inside ourselves. After each student has done an individual "Here and Now," you might ask them to collaborate on a composite, one that represents the major concerns of the group. You can then check the accuracy of your "Here and Now" about them by comparing it with the actual "Here and Now" provided by the students. With a colleague or small group of peers, or even with your students, you might then draw implications for your teaching from the information provided by a comparison between your expectations of their concerns and their actual concerns.

Student Use

As indicated above, "Here-and-Now" circles can be used to help us take account of our important concerns at any given time. If they are done repeatedly, we can keep a record of our concerns over a period of time; later we can look back to examine our lives. Students of junior-high-school age and older might be encouraged to keep such a record. Each time you ask them to do a "Here and Now," have them mark it with the date and the time. Also have them write a short paragraph explaining the concerns they included. Since many of our concerns are private, you must assure students that their "Here-and-Now" work need not be shared.

Students might also be interested in testing their ability to predict their future concerns. Have them select an event they are anticipating and do a "There and Then" that describes the concerns they anticipate at the future event. When the event happens, they should do a "Here and Now," which afterward can be compared with the "There and Then" done prior to the event. You will be able to spur some interesting and meaningful discussion on the predictability of human concerns, the possible external influences on them, and personal control over reactions and responses to external events.

VALUES IN THE CLASSROOM

Nearly all teaching behavior emanates from what we value as teachers. In making decisions, even in the case of instantaneous reflexive action, our values play a crucial role in determining the behavior we consider appropriate for a given moment. Values are one of the strongest influences on behavior. Yet how little we stop to think about which values are the most important in teaching, and how much less we consider how our behavior reflects our highest value priorities.

Teachers, of course, are not the only ones who often fail to relate values to behavior, but for us to ignore this relationship is to miss a crucial data source. Consider a teacher who says he values creativity more than he values peace and quiet. In actual practice this same teacher may ask his students to quiet down during a creative activity. What he says is not congruent with what he does. Of course he may be afraid of the principal's reaction to the noise or the reaction of the teacher next door, and thus another value-laden factor enters the situation. It appears, then, that he values the approval of the principal or colleague more highly than he values creativity.

While it is difficult always to act in accordance with our beliefs, we can be continually working toward a healthy integration of the two. The healthiest teacher is the one who is very close to having his behavior express his values. The following activity is a beginning toward identifying your value priorities and seeing how these priorities are reflected in your teaching.

Objectives

1. To list in order of importance the personal values that could influence your classroom.
2. To examine the list in terms of your observable classroom behavior.
3. To compare your values and behavior.

Directions

Below are twenty-two values that might be displayed in various ways in a classroom. In your ideal classroom, how would you rank them? Place a 1 next to the quality you value most in your classroom, a 2 next to the second most important, and so on through 22, which will represent the quality you value least.

_____Freedom	_____Dogmatism
_____Rigidity	_____Orderliness
_____Self-direction	_____Favoritism
_____Disorder	_____Creativity

_____Quiet	_____Alienation
_____Chaos	_____Respect
_____Laughter	_____Privacy
_____Passivity	_____Equality
_____Concentration	_____Dominance
_____Fear	_____Fairness
_____Purposefulness	_____Love

On the accompanying worksheet list the values you ranked in the top three positions. For each value list *three* classroom indicators that demonstrate the presence of that value in a classroom. Then list the values you ranked in the bottom three positions, and list for each one three classroom indicators that reflect that value in a classroom.

For example, if *freedom* is on your list, you might select the following as classroom indicators:

1. Students have an open reading list and read books on their own.
2. Students interact with one another without stimulus from teacher.
3. Teacher does not give tests or grades.

If *dogmatism* is on your list, you might select the following as classroom indicators:

1. Teacher gives only one choice of course readings.
2. Teacher asks for no student input into course curriculum.
3. Students do not initiate any classroom activities.

Questions

1. What specifically can you do to insure that the nine classroom indicators that represent your three highest-ranked values are incorporated into your classroom daily?
2. What can you do to insure that the nine classroom indicators of your three lowest-ranked values are eliminated from (or never introduced into) your classroom?
3. What values, other than those listed, are important to you? You might wish to add a number of your values to the previous list of

Worksheet

Values Ranked in Top Three Positions

1. _____[value]_____

   classroom indicator:

   classroom indicator:

   classroom indicator:

2. _____

   classroom indicator:

   classroom indicator:

   classroom indicator:

3. _____

   classroom indicator:

   classroom indicator:

   classroom indicator:

Worksheet

Values Ranked in Bottom Three Positions

1. _____[value]_____

   classroom indicator:

   classroom indicator:

   classroom indicator:

2. _____

   classroom indicator:

   classroom indicator:

   classroom indicator:

3. _____

   classroom indicator:

   classroom indicator:

   classroom indicator:

twenty-two, rank them again, and compare the results with your earlier ranking.

4. What values on the new list are too important for compromise? Which would you try to preserve at the cost of your job?

Follow-up

Give an observer your two lists with the nine positive indicators and the nine negative indicators. Have the observer watch you teach a variety of lessons and write down every instance of one of your eighteen indicators. Try to act as naturally as possible with the observer present. If you change your classroom actions because of the presence of the observer, the activity will be less helpful.

After you have completed a variety of lessons, examine the data collected by your observer and compare the collected data with your answers to the questions above. If your actions were not congruent with your stated values, then reevaluate your value priorities or change your behavior in relation to your stated values. This follow-up activity can be done at various times throughout the year for constant feedback.

Student Use

You may do this activity with your students by first listing the values that are possibly related to an aspect of student life. Such aspects are the school, the home, social life, and sports. A list for high-school-age students concerned with how they relate socially might look like the following:

SOCIAL LIFE

_____Honest	_____Caring
_____Consistent	_____Looking out for self
_____Private	_____Open
_____Generous	_____Contradictory
_____Protective	_____Unpredictable
_____Blunt	_____Deliberate
_____Straightforward	_____Spur of the moment
_____Gentle	_____Covetous
_____Subtle	_____Competitive

The students can add any additional appropriate values. Each student then ranks the values and lists behavior indicators that reflect his top three and bottom three values. The students then observe each other to check on the congruence between their stated values and their behavior. Students can keep journals of how they feel about the discrepancies between how they *want* to be and how others *see* them as being. The insights they gain from the comparison should be included.

LOG CONVERSATION: CONFORMITY AND CREATIVITY

Barbara: I've been thinking a lot lately about the kinds of environments that encourage creativity. While relating the findings of a committee of the Association of Supervision and Curriculum Development, Art Combs pointed out:

> For conformity and creativity are essentially antithetical—what produces one tends to destroy the other. Conformity calls for restriction, order, direction, control; creativity for freedom, experimentation, expression and facilitation. Teachers who want creativity can count on it —their classrooms will not be neat, quiet and orderly. Administrators who demand rigid conformity can count on it—their students will not be very creative, except possibly in devising ways to circumvent controls. The public, demanding more genius and creativity, on the one hand, and more rigid control, less "frills" and less expense, on the other, must also face the fact it cannot have both simultaneously. Whatever choice we make is going to cost us something. The choice will be hard, for some of the things we must give up are dear to our hearts and our pocketbooks. Nevertheless, a choice has to be made either for institutional order and dogmatism or for flexibility and freedom. Both conformity and creativity cannot grow in the same school atmosphere or classroom climate.[2]

What factors have you noticed as being common to creative environments?

Rick: For me the most important aspect of the environment of a creative classroom is a high level of trust and caring. Then people can experiment freely without fear of implicit or explicit judgments. What do our readers see as most important?

[2] A. W. Combs, ed., *Perceiving, Behaving, Becoming: A New Focus for Education,* 1962 ASCD Yearbook (Washington, D.C.: Association for Supervision and Curriculum Development, 1962), p. 144.

You:

Barbara: It's the teacher's responsibility to supply a creative environment. What have you done, Rick, to build a high level of trust and caring in your classrooms?

Rick: Well, I've encouraged discussion around questions and issues that have no right or wrong answers. My students spend much of their time in small groups. I also try to facilitate the development of students' ideas rather than always espousing my own. I wonder what our readers have done to develop the characteristics they consider important?

You:

Barbara: As I think back on my days in elementary and secondary school, I don't recall many creative or very enjoyable activities. I do recall a fun circus we put on in the first grade and a great group mural done in about the seventh grade, but most of my creative times were outside of school. I hope my son finds more in school than I did.

TWENTY THINGS YOU DID

Every teacher has a wealth of resources that can be used to gain insights into teaching. One resource that is common to all of us is *past experience,* but it is not used explicitly as a resource very often. Most of us do, in fact, respond to new teaching situations in light of our past experience as students. Unfortunately our past experience usually influences our behavior without our conscious awareness of its intervention. Being unaware, we let our past experience mold our behavior rather than using it as a basis for selecting appropriate behavior. We can control its influence, however, through a systematic examination of our past experience that focuses on its implications for current and future teaching. The fact that each of us has chosen the teaching profession indicates that past moments in the classroom have indeed had an effect on our attitudes, beliefs, values, and ideas about teaching. The following activity can help you use your past experience so that it can have immediate and specific applications to your teaching.

Objectives

1. To review past classroom experiences in a systematic manner.
2. To interpret data from past experiences to gain insight regarding our teaching effectiveness.
3. To compare past data with present teaching practices.

Directions

Imagine yourself back in school at the age of your students, in the class most like the one you are now or will be teaching—elementary reading, fourth grade, junior-high social studies, high-school science—whatever is appropriate for you. Think about all the things you did in that class or grade.

On the accompanying Worksheet 1, list twenty things you did in that class—wrote book reports, memorized the multiplication tables, whatever comes to mind as you recall your experiences. Choose activities that were related to instruction in some way. Do not, for example, include such activities as note-passing, spitball-throwing, or doodling. You may include spontaneous activities that were not preplanned by the teacher, or those initiated by students. Then read the evaluative codes across the top of the worksheet and add any appropriate codes that are not included in the spaces provided. Finally, check one or more of the boxes under the codes that describe each activity.

Questions

1. What is there in common among the activities you most enjoyed? least enjoyed?
2. What is there in common among the activities you found most helpful? least helpful?
3. Which categories seem to go together? (Did you notice that certain categories are usually checked in conjunction with other categories?)
4. Draw some conclusions from your experience that can influence your current teaching.
5. What activities will you use differently as a result of the implications drawn from the analysis of the worksheet?

Follow-up

Select some recent lessons that you have taught. You might use your plan book if you have recorded any of your lessons. Try to include a

	enjoyed activity	disliked activity	did activity alone	needed other people	involved rote learning	required imagination	long-term project	short-term project	exciting	boring
1.										
2.										
3.										
4.										
5.										
6.										
7.										
8.										
9.										
10.										
11.										
12.										
13.										
14.										
15.										
16.										
17.										
18.										
19.										
20.										

totally teacher-assigned	was helpful to my life	was fun but not too useful	would have been useful with any teacher	would have been useful with certain teachers only	outdoors	indoors	needed special room or equipment	could be done anywhere	required certain prerequisites	needed no prerequisites	was optional	was required	would never use in teaching	am using/will use

	enjoyed activity	disliked activity	did activity alone	needed other people	involved rote learning	required imagination	long-term project	short-term project	exciting	boring
1.										
2.										
3.										
4.										
5.										
6.										
7.										
8.										
9.										
10.										
11.										
12.										
13.										
14.										
15.										
16.										
17.										
18.										
19.										
20.										

totally teacher-assigned	was helpful to my life	was fun but not too useful	would have been useful with any teacher	would have been useful with certain teachers only	outdoors	indoors	needed special room or equipment	could be done anywhere	required certain prerequisites	needed no prerequisites	was optional	was required	would never use in teaching	am using/will use

wide variety of lessons, including some that were effective and some that were not so effective. List the lessons on Worksheet 2. Check the categories just as you did on the first worksheet, but as you check them this time, try to imagine how your students perceived the lesson. Check the categories from your feeling of how they would respond.

Compare the two worksheets by answering the following questions:

1. Are there any similarities between the two sets of twenty activities?
2. Are there any categories that are singularly appropriate for the lessons on your lists?
3. Do certain activities make particular lessons more effective?
4. Did the lessons that were not effective have anything in common? How can you avoid these common elements in the future?

The next time you plan a lesson, take out your worksheets and the answers to the above questions. Before you plan the lesson, examine the data. Then try to include in your lesson some of the qualities that are positive for you. When the lesson has been taught, you might find it enlightening to give your students a copy of the worksheets and let them check the boxes they feel are appropriate to your lesson. Their responses will be interesting and useful feedback for future lesson-planning.

Student Use

An ideal application of this activity is "Twenty Loves," which we learned from Sidney B. Simon at the University of Massachusetts in Amherst.

On a piece of paper have your students number from one to twenty. Then have them list twenty things in their lives that they love to do, very specific things that they have actually done. You might spur their thinking by offering a few items that you would include in your list of twenty: answering the phone, camping in the mountains, whatever. Next to each one—

1. place the date when you did it last;
2. place an *A* or *P* if you like to do it alone or *with* people;
3. place a $ sign if it costs more than five dollars to do it;
4. place an asterisk (*) by the five that you love the most;
5. check the items that would not have been there five years ago;
6. place an *R* next to those items that involve risk;
7. place an *I* for inside or an *O* for outside beside each item;

8. place an *M* for mother if the item is something that your mother would have liked, an *F* if your father would have liked it, and *MF* if both would have liked it.

Elementary children can list from four to ten things they love to do. This can be a very personal activity, and as in all valuing techniques, pupils should have the alternative of passing when asked to share.

LOG CONVERSATION: TEACHER ENERGY

Rick: Do you know that George Leonard claims in *Education and Ecstasy* that teachers dam up the flood of human potential?

Teachers are overworked and underpaid. True. It is an exacting and exhausting business, this damming up the flood of human potentialities. What energy it takes to make a torrent into a trickle, to train that trickle along narrow, well-marked channels! Teachers are often tired. In the teachers' lounge, they sigh their relief into stained cups of instant coffee and offer gratitude to whoever makes them laugh at the day's disasters. This laughter permits momentary, sanity-saving acknowledgement, shared by all, that what passes for humdrum or routine or boring is, in truth, tragic. (An hour, of which some fifty minutes are given up to "classroom control." One child's question unanswered, a hundred unasked. A smart student ridiculed: "He'll learn better." He learns.) Sweet laughter, shooting up like artesian water, breaks through encrusted perceptions and leaves a tear in a teacher's eye. A little triumph.[3]

Rick: I consider that a devastating statement. I'd like to know what immediate reactions you, our readers, have to this quotation.

You:

Barbara: I have to admit that I've seen a lot of teachers who spend enormous energy channeling students into routines. I've also seen a few who somehow manage to release and nourish their students' energies. I know, for example, a history teacher who doesn't allow discussion of im-

[3] George B. Leonard, *Education and Ecstasy* (New York: Delacorte, 1968), pp. 1–2. Reprinted by permission of the publisher.

portant current events such as a political assassination because they have to "cover" history, but I also know an English teacher who doesn't distribute books until the second month of class. She prefers to spend the first month helping her students learn how to interact with each other and how to release their creativity. I wonder if you, our readers, can recall teachers, both those you knew as students and those you've taught with, who restricted their students and those who nourished them. Which kind has been more prevalent in your experience?

You:

Rick: Reading Leonard's statement makes me want to learn how to help students release their energies. What suggestions do you have?

Barbara: One thing I encourage is the free exchange of ideas, especially far-out or half-formed ideas. That way students use each others' ideas as stimuli for their own. What suggestions do you, our readers, have?

You:

PERSONAL PLAQUE FOR TEACHERS

An interesting and enjoyable method of broadening the perspective of our teaching selves is through the use of symbolism. Most of us who have become teachers, or are in the process of becoming teachers, are comfortable and familiar with language. We can often ease in and out of situations that call for a facility with words. When we are asked to think in new symbols, our imagery is opened to a broader range of expression. The personal plaque is designed to have you consider in symbolic terms an overall view of your teaching self. You will develop a series of personal symbols that will reflect your important concerns and will help to broaden your perspective.

Objective

To symbolize important aspects of your teaching self in picture form.

Directions

On the accompanying worksheet, or on a large piece of art paper, draw (words can be used only in Area 5) in each area a symbolic representation of the following:

Area 1.   Your greatest success as a teacher.

Area 2.   Your greatest failure as a teacher.

Area 3.   A value you wish all teachers would hold.

Area 4.   Something you would like to accomplish as a teacher if your success were guaranteed.

Area 5.   A memorial to you, erected by your students, including the three words you'd most like them to say of you.

The drawing need not be a work of art. You may be as elaborate or as simple as you wish. Stick figures are perfectly acceptable, as are more sophisticated forms of art work. The symbols are important, not the skill of the artistry.

If you are working by yourself, you may wish to share your plaque with an associate or your observer and discuss the different items, using the questions below as a guide. If you are working in a group, it's fun to tape each plaque on the wall and then go on a tour of the newly created art gallery. Remember that you need not explain any private aspect of your plaque, for the right of privacy must always be respected.

Questions

1. Which was the most difficult symbol to depict? Which was the easiest?

2. Which picture helped you recall the most vivid memories? Which the least?

3. Are there any pictures you do not wish to explain? Why?

4. Are there any pictures you strongly wish to tell about? Why?

5. Which of the symbols on your plaque would have been different one year ago?

Student Use

Students of all ages can draw their personal plaques. We have seen plaques used in kindergartens, high schools and colleges. Each student can

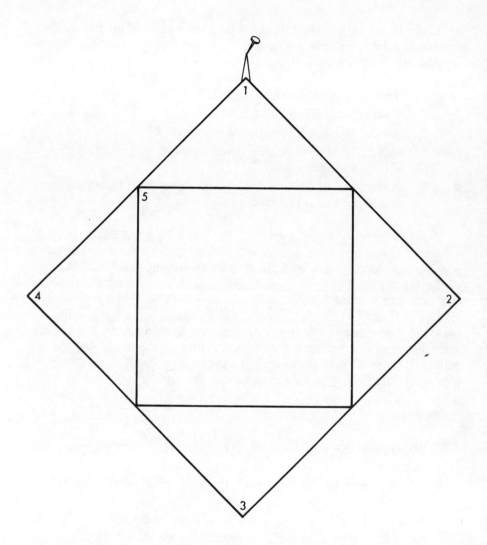

design the form and shape for his plaque and draw symbols for topics such as these:

Young people: Greatest success in school, greatest success at home, greatest failure in school or at home, biggest wish you hope will come true, one thing you would like to learn how to do in the next year.

Adults: Greatest success from the time you were born until twelve years of age, greatest failure, greatest success from age twelve until now, greatest failure, one value you wish everyone would hold, one thing you would like to accomplish if you were guaranteed success, three words you would like said about you when you have left your school.

A gallery walk in school is usually an exciting and memorable event. The students might wish to make it a monthly part of the class, creating different plaques each time. At the end of the year the students will have a unique record of their growth and changes.

LOG CONVERSATION: DISCIPLINE

Rick: In *Reach, Touch, and Teach,* Terry Borton says in reference to discipline that—

> Freedom was the issue then, and still is. In some cities, they cane students into submission; in many places, they slap, shake, and shove them. In many more, teachers subdue kids with threats, sarcasm, and ridicule. Like beatings with a blackjack, these techniques crush but leave no marks the eye can see.[4]

One second-grade teacher I've seen refuses to call upon a student who misbehaves, regardless of how often he raises his hand, for a period of two or three weeks following the misbehavior. What a blow being ignored must be. Can you recall a situation in which you were ridiculed in school?

Barbara: My most vivid recollection is of being in sixth grade and having to sit next to the teacher's desk for a whole week as punishment for whispering to my friend. That was the most humiliating week of my life. What situations do you readers recall, and what effect did the ridicule have on you?

[4] Terry Borton, *Reach, Touch, and Teach* (New York: McGraw-Hill, 1970), pp. 151–52.

You:

Rick: I've seen many techniques that "crush but leave no marks the eye can see." Can you readers describe three such techniques?

You:

Barbara: I doubt if there are any situations in which ridicule is positive. What do you readers think?

You:

Rick: How might the issue raised in Borton's quotation specifically affect your behavior as a teacher?

You:

CLASSROOM MANAGEMENT: WHAT IS YOUR STYLE?

Whether you teach in a traditional setting or in one of the many variations being tried with youngsters of all ages, you "manage" that environment in one way or another. It is likely that your management style is uniquely yours. Unfortunately, however, many of us have adopted certain styles not through careful examination and selection of alternatives, but merely by imitation or by accident. This activity is designed to help you become better aware of how you manage your classroom.

Objectives

1. To be aware of the management techniques you use in your classroom.
2. To effectively examine your management style and compare it with others.

3. To determine the possible effects on students of various styles.

Directions

Use the statements headed, "Classroom Management Style," and the sorting board on p. 48 to get a better idea of your management style. First record each of the forty-six statements about management practices on small cards. Then with the sorting board before you, sort the cards into the seven categories it illustrates. The number of cards put into the seven categories follows this order—1, 4, 9, 18, 9, 4, and 1—ranging from *most characteristic* of your behavior (one card) in category *A* to *least characteristic* of your behavior (also one card) in category *G*. When you finish you will have a general ranking of the statements, those in categories *A* and *B* describing your most characteristic behaviors, those in categories *F* and *G* describing behaviors that are least characteristic of you. The remainder will be arranged somewhere between these extremes.

If you have difficulty ranking some behaviors, you might add the element of importance to your ranking. Then you will rank the behavior that is more significant for you higher than the one that is less significant. It may be that you would prefer to place three or five behaviors in category *A* or in category *G,* instead of one. At that point you will have to force yourself to decide which *one* of those three or five is of greatest importance and concern to you. *The statements must be grouped according to the group sizes indicated*: 1, 4, 9, 18, 9, 4, 1. To facilitate arrangement, place each card on the board as you read it, then rearrange the cards as you work. It is considerably easier to rearrange on the board than to try to organize all forty-six cards before placing them.

Classroom Management Style

1. Desks in my classroom are usually arranged in rows.
2. I encourage students to speak spontaneously, without necessarily raising their hands.
3. My students call me by my first name.
4. Papers being turned in follow a standard format in my classroom.
5. The bulletin boards in my classroom are usually decorated by me, rather than by the students.
6. I usually follow and complete my lesson plans.
7. Students in my class are expected to ask permission to leave the room.
8. I allow students to go to the bathroom at just about any time.

Sorting Board

	A		B
	Most ideal		
	(Most characteristic)		
	1 card		4 cards

C	D	E
9 cards	18 cards	9 cards

	F	G
		Least ideal
		(Least characteristic)
	4 cards	1 card

9. My students may chew gum and eat most of the time.
10. My students usually sit in assigned places.
11. I often threaten punishment of one kind or another for misbehavior.
12. I frequently contact parents.
13. I do not tolerate swearing or other unacceptable language in my classroom.
14. When I monitor a study period, the students are quiet.
15. I often stand or sit behind a lecturn or desk when teaching.
16. My students and I sit on the floor.
17. Students often remove their shoes in my class.
18. I believe in reasonable dress codes for students and teachers.
19. Students probably consider me traditional.
20. My principal probably considers me traditional.
21. I encourage students to work independently in self-directed activities.
22. The students in my class make decisions about classroom management.
23. I often depart from or discard my lesson plans.
24. I sometimes keep students after school when they misbehave.
25. I tell my students a great deal about myself.
26. Students' questions sometimes frighten me.
27. I find it difficult to say "I don't know."
28. I often ask students for feedback concerning my teaching.
29. I am likely to be asked to keep my students quieter.
30. My classroom would probably be classified as teacher-oriented.
31. I am likely to be asked by students to attend or chaperone their parties.
32. I am likely to be advising student groups, formally or informally.
33. I laugh a lot in class.
34. I enjoy team-teaching.
35. I am careful about checking attendance.
36. I usually reprimand students who are tardy.
37. I get tense when my principal comes into my room.
38. I probably let students take advantage of me.
39. I enjoy being friends with my students.
40. I frequently touch students.
41. I expect respect from students.
42. I have carefully read my students' cumulative records.

43. I feel and act differently with students outside of class.
44. I sometimes send students to see the principal, vice-principal, or counselor when they misbehave.
45. I sometimes use sarcasm to win a point with a student.
46. I often sit on the desk.

Questions

1. What makes the statement in *A* so characteristic of you?
2. Do the statements in *B* have anything in common with one another? If so, what?
3. How are the statements in *A* and *B* similar for you?
4. Do the statements in *C* have anything in common with one another? If so, what?
5. How are the statements in *C* similar to or different from those in *A* and *B*?
6. As a result of your examination of the statements in *A, B,* and *C,* write five statements with this beginning: "I manage—."
7. What makes the statement in *G* so uncharacteristic of you?
8. Do the statements in *F* have anything in common with one another? If so, what?
9. How are the statements in *F* and *G* similar for you?
10. Do the statements in *E* have anything in common with one another? If so, what?
11. How are the statements in *E* similar to or different from those in *F* and *G*?
12. As a result of your examination of the statements in *E, F,* and *G,* write five statements with this beginning: "I generally do not—."
13. Based on the information drawn from the sorting activity above, write a paragraph describing the characteristics and behaviors of your personal style of classroom management.

Follow-up

If you have the opportunity to work with a support group, you might use the group to discuss and compare your individual styles of classroom management. After sharing the paragraphs you wrote following the sorting activity, discussion might focus on the following questions:

1. In what ways are your various styles of classroom management similar? Are your similarities based on a common belief, on habit, or on some other factor?

2. In what ways do your styles differ? Are your differences important? Do you need to work them out? If not, why not? If so, why?
3. What are students likely to learn about each of you as a result of the way you manage your classroom? Are you pleased about what they may be learning?
4. Have you identified any behavior that you would like to change? If so, share your concerns with the other group members and elicit their help in designing a plan that will help you change.

Student Use

You may wish to devise for students of junior-high-school age and older a sorting activity that compares their attitudes with their behavior (see "Classroom Management: What Is Your Style?," pp. 46–51). (Children younger than junior-high-school age might have difficulty with the sorting concept underlying the activity and might become so involved with the mechanics that they would miss the meaning of the activity. However, you could use the basic design—a comparison of beliefs with actions on some subject of concern to the children—and create an activity around it.)

From your experience and the concerns expressed by your students, select an issue and write a number of position statements concerning that issue for the first half of the activity. (We used forty-six statements, but you may use less or more as long as the number can be conveniently divided into such categories as those on the sorting board. Note that the number of statements assigned to each category approximates a normal distribution.) For example, you could devise an activity concerning the issue of *honesty*. Position statements that indicate moral rightness or wrongness could include such statements as the following:

It's OK to lie to spare someone's feelings.

It's OK to lie to get out of trouble.

Insincerity is as dishonest as lying.

It's better to tell the truth, no matter what the consequences.

When a store clerk gives you too much change, it's her fault, so it's OK to keep it.

A fib is permissible; a lie is not.

These should be sorted along a continuum ranging from "most ideal" to "least ideal." Follow the statements with appropriate questions to help students analyze their attitudes toward honesty and dishonesty; then design a list of statements referring to *specific past or recurring behaviors* for use in the second half of this activity. These might look like the following:

> I have told someone what that person wanted to hear rather than what I really thought.
>
> I have distorted the truth rather than be punished.
>
> I have never copied another person's homework.
>
> I have kept extra change mistakenly given to me.

These statements should be sorted along the range "most characteristic of me" to "least characteristic of me." Then follow them with appropriate discussion questions, including comparison of the results of the two sortings, and finally with some means of translating any learning that resulted into future action. Of course, as with any activity that asks students to critically examine their attitudes and behaviors, students must be assured that their responses may remain private. They need not share responses or learning with anyone.

LOG CONVERSATION: GRADING

Barbara: Grading has become a hot issue in recent years. Paul Dressel contends that "A grade [is] an inadequate report of an inaccurate judgment by a biased and variable judge of the extent to which a student has attained an undefined level of mastery of an unknown proportion of an indefinite amount of material." [5] Wow! To me that says we have absolutely *no* basis for giving grades. Where do you stand on this issue, Rick?

Rick: I consider grades one of the biggest hindrances to learning ever devised. I think they must be totally eliminated if learning is to occur. I wonder if our readers can make positive statements that define their positions on the issue.

You:

Barbara: Rick, I know that you are working toward the elimination of grades in your classes. I also know many people who believe, with strong reason and conviction, that grades are necessary; and they are acting to institute or maintain an equitable grading system. Regardless of what your particular position is, what have you readers done to support your position? What *will* you do?

[5] Paul Dressel, *Basic College Quarterly*, Michigan State University.

You:

EVALUATION OF STUDENTS: WHERE DO YOU STAND?

Part One

How many of the routine practices that you have initiated in your classroom have you thoroughly considered before doing? Most of us carefully analyze some of our practices, think sketchily about others, and consider some not at all. We have been learning teaching behavior all our lives: from our parents (our first and most pervasive teachers), our elementary and secondary teachers, our college instructors, our cooperating teachers and supervisors, and our colleagues. Frequently, however, we fail to think very deeply about whether or not this learned behavior truly constitutes our ideal conception of what teaching behavior ought to be. The following activity gives you an opportunity to think about your beliefs and attitudes as they relate to the matter of evaluating students.

Objectives

1. To examine your beliefs about evaluating students.
2. To evaluate your practices in evaluating students.

Directions

Use the statements headed, "Attitudes on Evaluation," and the sorting board on p. 48 to describe your conception of "good" and "not-so-good" practices related to evaluation. First record the forty-six attitude statements on small cards. With the sorting board before you, sort the cards into seven categories, with 1, 4, 9, 18, 9, 4, and 1 statements in each of the respective categories, ranging from "most ideal" in category *A* to "least ideal" in category *G*. When you finish, you will have a general ranking of the statements. Those in categories *A* and *B* describe what you believe to be sound evaluative practices; those in categories *F* and *G* describe what you believe to be unsound practices, with the remainder ranging somewhere between the extremes. Place each card on the board as you read it and rearrange the cards as you work.

Attitudes on Evaluation

1. It's best to consider and take into account a student's intelligence when evaluating his work.
2. Final exams or unit tests demonstrate competence and should contribute significantly to a student's evaluation.
3. The amount of effort a student expends should be reflected in his evaluation.
4. A student's progress during a specified marking period is measured well by a single major performance criterion, usually a test of some kind.
5. A student's ability to relate to others is an important factor and should be considered when evaluating him.
6. A student's willingness to contribute to class discussion and activity should be considered when evaluating him.
7. The feelings evoked in the teacher by a student are significant measures of the student's competency and should be considered in the teacher's evaluation.
8. A student's willingness and ability to follow the teacher's directions are important measures of his competency and should be considered in the teacher's evaluation.
9. Students should be discouraged from taking issue with teachers.
10. Using a standard curve is the fairest way to evaluate students.
11. A student's ability to be creative is an important measure of his competency, so creative activities should be evaluated.
12. The ability to communicate clearly in writing is of great importance, so the way a student writes should be considered more important than what he writes.
13. Students generally achieve more if they are faced with challenges, so it is best not to give too many A's or superior evaluations.
14. Students need positive reinforcement in order to go beyond where they are, so it is best not to fail students.
15. Because students often are not motivated to work outside the classroom, it is a good idea to suggest that they will be quizzed on homework assignments.
16. Student opinion and interpretation are significant means and indications of learning and should be emphasized in tests and other methods of evaluation.
17. Students will not be able to apply knowledge until they have

mastered the basics, so tests and other means of evaluation should emphasize the acquisition of factual material.

18. Because what a student knows is more important than how well he is able to communicate it in writing, content rather than style or grammar should be emphasized in students' writing.

19. Because it is important for students to learn to spell well, students should be penalized for spelling errors.

20. Good spelling is an asset and therefore should be encouraged by giving students extra points on tests and papers for perfect spelling.

21. Quizzes and tests that are unannounced are better measures of actual learning than those that are announced in advance.

22. Neatness should be encouraged by giving it consideration when evaluating student work.

23. Low grades and poor evaluations usually create incentives for students to work harder.

24. It is often helpful to solicit the opinions of other teachers about the students and to consider these opinions when evaluating the students.

25. High grades and good evaluations usually create incentive for students to work harder.

26. Students will work harder if they feel their work is appreciated, so it is helpful to openly appreciate what they do.

27. Because students should know where they stand in relation to other students, all grades should be public.

28. To de-emphasize grades, it is good practice not to tell a student what his grades are until the end of the term, when the school administration insists that they be shared.

29. Promptness should be encouraged by penalizing students for tardiness.

30. It is a significant learning experience for students to be allowed and encouraged to negotiate their evaluations with teachers.

31. Students contracting with teachers for grades prior to a unit of work is a meaningful, fair, and positive way to handle evaluation.

32. It is best to give many more positive than negative evaluations.

33. It is better to consistently criticize student work than to consistently praise it.

34. The last day of the week is a good time to evaluate students' progress for that week.

35. In order that students not lose ground over vacation periods, it is a good idea to assign homework then.

36. A good teacher should be accountable for the performance of his students.
37. Tests should be used diagnostically rather than evaluatively.
38. Standard grading procedures are generally detrimental and should be eliminated.
39. Alternatives to standard grading procedures should be explored and tried.
40. The parents of students who are not doing well should be notified.
41. All parents should be notified of their children's progress in school.
42. Teachers should be concerned about cheating.
43. Students who miss tests should be required to complete more difficult makeup work.
44. Students should be allowed and encouraged to evaluate themselves.
45. Students should be allowed and encouraged to evaluate one another.
46. A student's sex should be considered in evaluating his work.

Questions

After you have sorted the ideal evaluative practices, answer the following questions:

1. What makes the statement in *A* so meaningful for you?
2. Do the statements in *B* have anything in common with one another? If so, what?
3. How are the statements in *A* and *B* similar for you?
4. Do the statements in *C* have anything in common with one another? If so, what?
5. How are the statements in *C* similar to or different from those in *A* and *B*?
6. As a result of your examination of the statements in *A, B,* and *C,* complete five statements beginning with the words "I believe—."
7. What makes the statement in *G* so unacceptable to you?
8. Do the statements in *F* have anything in common with one another? If so, what?
9. How are the statements in *F* and *G* similar for you?

10. Do the statements in *E* have anything in common with one another? If so, what?

11. How are the statements in *E* similar to or different from those in *F* and *G*?

12. As a result of your examination of the statements in *E, F,* and *G,* complete five more statements beginning with the words "I believe——."

13. Based on the information drawn from the sorting activity above, write a paragraph describing the characteristics and behavior concerning evaluation that are important to you.

Part Two

How consistent with your statements of belief is your actual behavior? All of us at times fail to act on our beliefs, sometimes because we have not truly incorporated the beliefs we profess, other times because we have not consciously related our behavior to our professed beliefs. Sometimes we fail because we hold conflicting beliefs, and other times because it is simply easier to act inconsistently with beliefs, even though we are uncomfortable doing so. No matter how difficult it is to act in a way that is congruent with our beliefs, it is certainly worthwhile to work toward this kind of consistency in life. One of the hallmarks of the healthiest people in all societies is the congruence of their values, attitudes, beliefs, and behavior.

In part one of this activity you examined your attitudes and beliefs as they relate to evaluating students. Now we ask you to describe your actual behavior in a similar fashion.

Objectives

1. To describe your behavior concerning the evaluation of students.
2. To compare your behavior with your stated beliefs.
3. To determine if new behavior or a reconsideration of beliefs might be appropriate for you, and to determine what these might be.

Directions

As before, record the statements headed "Evaluation Practices" on cards; then shuffle and sort them in the same manner as you did in Part One, but this time ranging from "most characteristic" to "least characteristic" of you in the classroom. These statements all contain the personal pronoun *I* and are meant to describe your actual behavior.

Evaluation Practices

1. I grade slower students differently from bright ones.
2. I weigh final exams and unit tests heavily, using them for fifty percent or more of a student's grade.
3. I give better evaluations to those who try harder.
4. I usually give one major test or other measure of evaluation each marking period.
5. I have been influenced in my evaluation of a student by how well he gets along with his peers.
6. Students who participate actively in class receive better evaluations from me than those who do not.
7. I trust my personal feelings for students and frequently use them to evaluate students.
8. I have graded students who agree with me differently from those who do not.
9. I have encouraged my students to disagree with me in class.
10. I use a standard grading curve in assigning grades.
11. I have used letter- or number-grades in evaluating creative activities.
12. I have given considerable weight to the grammatical correctness of student papers.
13. I did not give very many A's or superior evaluations last term.
14. I did not fail anyone last term.
15. I have used the threat of unannounced quizzes to motivate students to do homework.
16. Most of my tests rely on subjective questions that allow student opinion and interpretation.
17. Most of my test questions are objective, requiring students to respond with factual material.
18. In evaluating student work, I consider content more heavily than style or the correctness of usage.
19. I usually take points off a paper that contains numerous misspelled words.
20. I have given extra points to papers with no spelling errors.
21. I have given surprise quizzes.

22. I have lowered the evaluation of a paper because it was messy.

23. I have sometimes given students lower evaluations than I might have in order to motivate them to work harder.

24. I have sought out and listened to my colleagues' opinions about students when determining how to evaluate them.

25. I have given students higher grades than I might have in order to motivate them to work harder.

26. I have personally thanked or otherwise expressed my appreciation to students who have done excellent work.

27. I have posted or publicly announced student evaluations.

28. I have kept all grades and evaluations secret from students until the end of the marking period.

29. I have lowered the evaluation of a student paper or project for being turned in late.

30. I have negotiated with students for their evaluations, and both student and teacher have been satisfied with the final decision.

31. I have written grading contracts with students prior to a unit of work and have honored the contracts.

32. My students probably consider me an easy grader.

33. My students probably consider me a hard grader.

34. I frequently give exams or other means of evaluation on Fridays.

35. I have never assigned homework over a vacation period.

36. I have felt personally responsible for the poor performance of a student of mine.

37. I have used tests diagnostically; I have given tests before the end of a term, and without grading them, have used them to plan for future activities.

38. I have used other than standard grading procedures and have worked in my school to make them acceptable.

39. I have looked for and considered alternate grading systems to the generally accepted ones.

40. I have sent progress reports to parents of students doing poorly.

41. I have sent progress reports to parents of all students.

42. I have taken specific measures to prevent cheating in my classes.

43. I have given makeup tests that have been purposely more difficult than the original.

44. I have allowed students to grade themselves on a project or for a term.

45. I have allowed students to grade one another on a project or for a term.
46. I have at times been influenced by the sex of my students in determining their evaluations.

Questions for Analysis

1. What makes the statement in *A* so meaningful for you?
2. Do the statements in *B* have anything in common with one another? If so, what?
3. How are the statements in *A* and *B* similar for you?
4. Do the statements in *C* have anything in common with one another? If so, what?
5. How are the statements in *C* similar to or different from those in *A* and B?
6. As a result of your examination of the statements in *A, B,* and *C,* complete five statements beginning with the words "I am—."
7. What makes the statement in *G* so unacceptable to you?
8. Do the statements in *F* have anything in common with one another? If so, what?
9. How are the statements in *F* and *G* similar for you?
10. Do the statements in *E* have anything in common with one another? If so, what?
11. How are the statements in *E* similar to or different from those in *F* and G?
12. As a result of your examination of the statements in *E, F,* and *G,* complete five more statements beginning with "I am—."
13. Based on the information drawn from the sorting activity above, write a paragraph describing the characteristics and behavior concerning your procedures of evaluation.

Follow-up

You now have two profiles, one that states your beliefs concerning the evaluation of students, another that enumerates your actual classroom practices. Compare the two, using the following questions as a guide.

1. What strong similarities exist between the two profiles? In what ways are your beliefs and behaviors congruent?
2. In what ways are the two profiles different? How are your beliefs and behaviors incongruent?

3. Would you be willing to reconsider any of your stated beliefs? If so, which?

4. In light of your stated beliefs, would you be willing to reconsider any of your behavior?

5. Write a contract with yourself about something you will do to make your beliefs and behavior more congruent when it comes to evaluating students.

WHOM WOULD YOU HIRE?

What personal and professional characteristics do you believe are most important for effective teachers? How much does experience contribute to a teacher's skill? Do you feel that younger teachers are generally better than older ones? Of what importance is a teacher's personal life outside the classroom? Are the sex and race of a prospective teacher worth considering?

These questions and others like them are of considerable importance to the administrators whose responsibility it is to hire faculty for their schools. However, teachers and prospective teachers are seldom, if ever, asked to seriously consider the qualities that contribute to effective teaching, and even less frequently to analyze how their professional and personal characteristics compare either with their ideal or with the ideals of others. The following activity is designed to provide you with experience in analyzing the possible effectiveness of various personal and professional characteristics.

Objectives

1. To consider the possible effects on teaching quality of various personal and professional characteristics.

2. To examine the process of selecting from various candidates those who might provide the most effective teaching staff.

3. To examine your beliefs in relation to those of others through negotiation in a small group.

4. To further develop your group-process skills.

Directions

Imagine that you are an elementary-school administrator with responsibility for hiring new teachers. You have four positions open in grades one through three and eight applicants from whom to choose. You have interviewed all eight, each of whom impressed you favorably. Read through the brief descriptions below and select the four you would hire. (Admittedly these sketches are briefer than you would have in reality, but no matter how much material you have, it would undoubtedly never be enough.)

Candidate 1: Forty-year-old female, single, lives alone. Eighteen years' outstanding experience, highly successful with typically unsuccessful students. Possible lesbian relationships.

Candidate 2: Twenty-four-year-old male, single, two years' experience in ghetto school. Near genius, outstanding recommendations. Leader of local black-power group; his students use African names and openly reject "slave" names.

Candidate 3: Thirty-five-year-old male, married, father of six. Community-minded, interested in Cub Scouts. Known for having very well-organized, planned lessons and classes. Ten years' experience.

Candidate 4: Forty-year-old male, single, living with aged parents. Extensive experience as local businessman before returning to college for credentials. Just completed requirements, and received $5,000 grant to work with junior-high-school students in distributive education.

Candidate 5: Twenty-six-year-old female, divorced, supporting self and three small children alone. Highly creative; three years' experience; outstanding recommendations on professional capability.

Candidate 6: Forty-eight-year-old male, highly respected former minister who left pulpit to work full time with children. Has just completed teaching credentials.

Candidate 7: Fifty-eight-year-old female, widowed. Twenty-five years' experience, including three years in the Infant Schools of England. Wants to incorporate Infant-School concepts here.

Candidate 8: Twenty-two-year-old female, single, one year experience, excellent recommendations. Voluntarily tutored all four years in college, including full time in the summers. Living openly in the community with a man of another race.

When you have selected four, collaborate with other members of your support group (three to six others in a group is preferable) in order to function as a personnel committee for the school you choose to represent. Establish ground rules for the operation of your committee, including a possible chairmanship, the decision-making process (majority vote or consensus), and whatever other considerations you feel important.

When your group has selected your new teachers, post your selections and compare your choices with those of other groups (if there are other groups). A spokesman for each group might summarize the reasoning behind each group's choices.

Questions

(*Answer both individually and as a group.*)

1. What qualities or characteristics in elementary teachers do you value most highly?
2. What qualities or values have little or no relevance for you?
3. Would your choices have been different for high-school teachers? How?
4. Were you protecting anything in yourself in the choices you made? If so, what? Do you want to continue protecting that?
5. How would you have fared in your committee if you had been one of the candidates?

Follow-up

(*Group process.*) Effective interaction in a group is itself a skill that warrants critical examination and can be learned. It is therefore helpful to look closely at our actions within groups in an attempt to bring into awareness our patterns of behavior. We want to be able to choose, and subsequently practice, the behavior that most facilitates effective group interaction.

One way to begin an examination of group effectiveness is first to scrutinize individual behavior. Analyze your own behavior along each of the following scales. Mark where you think your behavior could be best described along each continuum.

follower_____leader

listened
carefully to   rehearsed my own
others' opinions_____opinions

sought informa-   disregarded infor-
tion and opin-   mation and opinions
ions from others_____of others

gave in on
everything_____nothing

goal-oriented_____process-oriented

said what I   held back
thought_____thoughts

aggressive_____submissive

passive_____active

uncaring_____caring

If you have established rapport and understanding in your group, each of you may wish to share your responses to the scales above, asking other members of the group for feedback. Then answer for yourself the following questions:

1. Were there any scales on which your rating of yourself and that of others in your group differed significantly? How do you account for the difference?
2. On which of the scales are you satisfied with your behavior? On which did you discover something you would like to change?
3. What specifically can you do to move yourself in the desired direction on one of the scales? Write a contract with yourself about something you will do the next time you are in a group situation. Then, following that group situation, rate youself on the scale and analyze your success in honoring your contract.
4. Your behavior in a group is probably very much like your behavior in a classroom situation. For example, if you consistently listen carefully to the opinions of other group members, you probably also listen carefully to your students; if you are consistently a follower in a group situation, it is unlikely that you suddenly become an active leader when teaching. Look again at your self-ratings on the scales above. How well do they correspond with your picture of yourself as a teacher? What would you like to change? How can you change it?

Student Use

Any number of activities that require students to choose values can be devised and are appropriate for children of all ages. Three simple ground rules for creating such activities are all you need to get started.

1. All candidates should be equally positive *or* equally negative *or* should each possess both positive and negative characterisitics.
2. There are no wrong answers. Choices are based on personal beliefs and attitudes.
3. Students' rights to privacy and nonparticipation must be respected.

In creating activities, think of situations and characters that would have meaning for the children. Young children, for example, might be asked to choose from a list of possible camping bunkmates—those they would prefer to live with for a week. Older youngsters might select a specified number of individuals from a prospective guest list for a party; those they would be willing to spend a week with in a survival training program; those they would choose as a negotiating team for world peace; those teachers they would select to staff a hypothetical school.

THE FACULTY ROOM

The conversations and activities of people in the faculty room of any school reveal a great deal about what life is like in that school. For example, imagine the following teachers interacting in a typical faculty room:

Frantic Frances spends her free period madly putting together a lesson plan or just as madly grading papers that she promised to return last week. She chain-smokes, with most of her energy drained into tapping ashes and shuffling papers. She accomplishes little.

Quiet Calvin always occupies the chair in the far corner of the room. He spends the period reading the daily newspaper, and although friendly, seldom joins in a conversation.

Mouth Millie and *News Nellie* know and tell everything about every faculty member in the school district. In their hands, the slightest rumor becomes substantiated fact. They always plan their schedules in order to share free time during the school day.

Funny Fred thinks himself the humorist. He often makes comments like "Gee, Marge, I thought you were going to have your hair done," just after she obviously has. Or, in noticing Sue's new, very casual and "mod" pants outfit, he says, "When did you decide to be a student rather than a teacher?" He might also pull practical jokes, like hiding a grade book. Though others often laugh, they seldom share his joy in his humor.

Athlete Al organizes both students and faculty for athletic events. He's the guy in the faculty room who also knows all the latest scores and plays Monday-morning quarterback all week long. He manages the weekly sports pool.

Griping Gil complains continually—about students, faculty, administrators, the system, the town, the weather, his family, his car, and everything else.

Theoretic Theodore considers himself a sophisticated academic, particularly in the area of educational theory. In the faculty room he frequently tells others how they are doing things wrong, referring for support to the latest book he has read.

Harried Harriet dislikes students. She rushes into the faculty room, wringing her hands and proclaiming her need for coffee and a cigarette to soothe the nerves "those beasts" have jangled and frazzled.

Sunshine Sally is always bright, cheerful, and willing to take on added responsibilities. She is the one who always manages fund-raising activities and sees that faculty members who are ill receive flowers.

Stranger Stan avoids the faculty room, coming only when it becomes imperative to speak with someone who is there. He usually spends his free time working in his classroom.

1. Which of the above teachers are most like real people you know? What is your personal reaction to each of them?
2. If you walked into a faculty room in which the characters above were seated, whom would you prefer to sit near? Whom would you avoid?

3. Describe either yourself or a new character whom you would like to emulate.

Below is a list of topics that frequently are discussed in faculty rooms. Read them over and add any with which you are familiar that often surface in a faculty room. Then rank the list in terms of their frequency and importance in a faculty room you know. Place a *1* next to the topic most often heard and so on; the highest number goes to the item least often heard.

_____the administration	_____educational theory
_____troublesome students	_____personal health
_____good students	_____the school calendar
_____community concerns	_____night life
_____workload	_____sex
_____weather	_____jokes
_____sports	_____how many days left until—
_____TV	_____fashions
_____politics	_____student teachers in building
_____faculty meetings	_____money

Look carefully at the topics you ranked in the top four positions on your frequency list. What do these topics reveal about the interests and concerns of your faculty? How do these interests influence the school?

What topics would you *prefer* to be the most frequent topics of discussion in your faculty room, whether they are listed above or not? In the spaces below, indicate the four that you think would be the most profitable for your faculty room.

1.

2.

3.

4.

What, specifically, do you expect each of these four topics to generate in your faculty room?

Introduce the four topics you have identified into your faculty room conversations and keep a record of what happens over a period of a few weeks. Look over your record and answer the following questions:

1. Which topics were well-received? Which generated little or no interest?
2. Did any of the topics generate a different atmosphere in the faculty room? How?
3. What observations about your faculty room can you make as a result of this activity?

SCHOOL OF THE FUTURE

Anyone who tries to draw the future in hard lines and vivid hues is a fool. The future will never sit for a portrait. It will come around a corner we never noticed, take us by surprise. And yet, foolishly, I cannot deny a vision born of indignation and hope. George Sand has called indignation at what is wrong in humanity one of the most passionate forms of love. If this is so, hope for something better may be love of a most enduring sort. Kennedy School in Santa Fe, New Mexico, exists not in the blazing immediacy of the twenty-first century, but in the indignation and hope of today. If it should sound like science fiction, do not be misled. Everything there is technically feasible. We don't really have to wait until the year 2001; it is only people, their habits, their organizations that may take so long to move. The alternatives, real alternatives, exist now.[6]

With this statement George Leonard introduces his readers to his personal "school of the future," a school that projects into the twenty-first century and enables the children of that time to inhabit and control their environment.

Although we obviously cannot draw the future "in hard lines and vivid hues," we all have ideas and we all can become clearer in our understanding our needs. Projecting our own personal school of the future can help us focus on the individual components—physical needs, budget, and learning philosophy, for example—that make a school what it is. It can also help us clarify our views on each of those components.

If you enjoy writing, you may choose to write a description of your

---

[6] George Leonard, *Education and Ecstasy* (New York: Delacorte, 1968), pp. 139–40. Reprinted by permission of the publisher.

Basic philosophy and goals:

Curriculum:

Students:

Teachers (training, characteristics):

Administrative organization:

Schedule:

Equipment and supplies:

Budget (cost per student; sources of funding):

Taboos:

Other:

ideal school of the future. Use the list of components and influences on the accompanying worksheet to spur your thinking.

If you are not a writer, simply jot down on the worksheet your ideas concerning each of the areas. Note the space marked "Other" at the bottom of the page, where you can fill in any areas that we have overlooked. When you finish, you will have quite a complete outline of the major concerns on which your ideal school would be built.

When you have completed a written description or the worksheet, look over your school of the future and select two or three elements that you feel are of utmost importance. What makes these so very important to you? What can you do now or in the near future to bring them into existence for the students with whom you are working?

Students, too, have valuable ideas about what schools should be like. They also can grow significantly in their ability to work in small groups, as well as in their ability to conceptualize a total environment, by designing their school of the future. Adolescents can respond to the accompanying worksheet. For younger students, you may want to simplify the description and ask only for their ideas about an ideal building and grounds, subjects to be studied, equipment needed, major qualifications for teachers, and the most important purposes of the school. Creating the important rules and taboos of an ideal school might provide another activity for younger students. In any case, students will benefit most by working in small groups, with some attention paid to the processes they use to arrive at decisions.

BODY LANGUAGE

In our posture, facial expression, arm and leg positioning, and body movement, each of us conveys a great deal of information about our attitudes and feelings of the moment. Each of us also responds, consciously or unconsciously, to the posture, facial expression, arm and leg positioning, and body movements of others. For example, a person sitting in a corner with his legs tightly crossed, arms tightly folded, and head leaning forward so that his eyes are on the floor, tells me that he has withdrawn from whatever is occurring in the room. I am unlikely to approach him. But if he "opens up" by uncrossing his arms and legs, moving toward the center of the room, looking up and smiling, I will probably respond with friendly overtures.

Body language is more powerful than verbal language. If the message of the body conflicts with the verbal message, the body message usually prevails. How many times have you heard "She said she feels OK, but

I know she doesn't," or "He says he isn't angry any more, but his face is still red." If the person who is sitting in the corner with his arms and legs tightly crossed says he feels friendly, I am unlikely to believe him, for his body tells me a different story. As teachers, we must be aware of the messages we are conveying through our body language so that we can better understand the responses of our students to us.

Objectives

1. To be aware of the effects of body language.
2. To be sensitive to personal body messages.
3. To consciously control body messages in the classroom.

Directions

A. Each of the photographs on the next few pages shows a teacher in action. Study the pictures. What does the body language of each teacher tell you about his or her attitudes and feelings of the moment? Briefly describe the message each conveys to you. Then check your perceptions by comparing them with the perceptions of your colleagues.

B. Observe others carefully, noting particular messages conveyed through body language. For example, you might especially notice how people's hands tell stories about what is going on inside them. What does nail-biting tell you? What do you infer about a person who rubs his shoulder a great deal? One who uses his hands very expressively when discussing a particular subject? One who keeps his hands so tightly folded when in the company of another individual that his knuckles turn white? Record a series of your body-language observations until you feel relatively confident that you are aware of the significance of body language and that you can read it accurately.

C. If you have access to video-tape equipment, have someone video-tape you in class. A short ten-minute segment will be sufficient, but you can use a longer tape if you wish. Afterward, *with the sound turned off,* view the entire tape while stopping the action periodically. Each time you stop the action, answer the questions below. Then view the tape with the sound on to check the congruency of your body language with your verbal language.

Questions for each "still" or single observation:

1. What classroom event or exchange immediately preceded this slice of action?

What do you think these teachers are feeling? What messages are being conveyed?

What do you think these teachers are feeling? What messages are being conveyed?

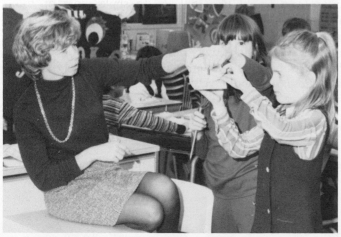

2. What message is conveyed by the position of your body? by the position of your arms and legs? by your facial expression?
3. Are you giving the same message to everyone in the class, or are some students getting a different message than others?
4. How congruent is your body language with your verbal language in this instance?
5. How did students respond?

If you do not have access to video-tape equipment, use an observer to record observations concerning your body language in the classroom. Observations should be specific, including preceding and succeeding classroom events, concurrent verbal messages, and student responses.

Questions

1. With which of the body messages you sent are you most pleased? How can you insure that you repeat similar messages?
2. With which of the body messages are you displeased? What can you do to avoid such messages in the future?

Follow-up

If you are working with a support group, you might choose to share your tapes or observation records with the group. Stop the action and look at individual messages in the group setting. Discussion should focus on helping one another identify positive aspects of body movement and developing means of improving in areas in which each individual asks for assistance. As with all other group activities, each individual has the unquestionable right not to participate.

When you have identified a body movement or habit that you would like to change (perhaps you would like to learn to smile more or to kneel more frequently so as to put yourself on eye level with children), specify some particular things you can do to accomplish your objective, and then get to work on them. Repeat the activity described above periodically (once a week for three weeks as a minimum) and focus your analysis on the behavior you have chosen to modify. Use your support group to help you as you deem necessary.

Student Use

Whether they are conscious of it or not, all students respond to body language and convey important messages with it. All students can become increasingly aware of how they use and respond to body language. Young children, as well as older ones, enjoy making faces and using their bodies to express emotions—angry, sad, happy, silly, embarrassed, shy—and usually revel in play-acting or miming events, either real or imagined, from their own experiences or from stories, novels, or factual accounts being studied in class. You can capitalize on their natural interest while increasing their awareness and control of their body language by allowing them every opportunity to use their bodies expressively. Discuss the effects of body language with them. You can also help them become aware of the messages they are sending by asking them questions or making comments, at appropriate times, like the following:

1. A young boy wrings his hands while telling you he lost his textbook. You might say, nonjudgmentally of course, "Are you aware of what you're doing with your hands?" or "I see you wringing your hands, and I imagine that you are upset."
2. A high-schoooler who has just been elected to a class office says he doesn't want to be so well-known but literally beams while saying so. You might say, "The sparkle in your eyes and your smile tell me you are really very pleased," or "Are you aware of the expression on your face right now?"
3. A third-grader with drooping shoulders tell you she has lost her lunch money. You might say, "Your body told me something was wrong. Now your words confirm it."

COMMUNICATING FEELINGS

Each of us, when we walk into the classroom, brings a host of experiences and feelings that significantly affect our behavior. It is simply impossible to turn off or tune out all the influences from our relationships and experiences outside the classroom. Often, too, we fail to allow into awareness the feelings that affect us. As a result, we frequently send mixed, ambiguous messages. Both our verbal and nonverbal behavior communicates to others—students as well as colleagues—what is going on inside, but it is usually difficult to interpret another's behavior accurately because feelings are seldom expressed clearly and unambiguously. The following activity is designed to increase your awareness of how feelings can affect your behavior and how well you perceive the motivation that underlies the behavior of others.

Objectives

1. To identify the feelings that are influencing the behavior of another person.
2. To be aware of how your feelings affect your behavior at any given moment.
3. To be able to identify the unstated messages that both you and others communicate.

Directions

1. Have each of the entries listed under "Role-Playing" copied on a card by someone who agrees to "sit this one out." Then shuffle the cards, but refrain from reading them. Turn the cards face down in a place convenient to all group members.
2. Designate an individual in your small group to begin. This person will role-play a teacher while the other group members role-play students of the age designated by the teacher. Teacher draws a card and role-plays greeting his class in the morning just after having experienced the situation and dominant emotion specified on the card.
3. The teacher may not share the experience itself with the students, but he may use any means he chooses to convey how he feels this morning.
4. Following the teacher's role-playing, each group member should write down on a worksheet similar to the sample on p. 77 a word or two that describes the feeling he thinks underlies the teacher's activity and the behavior that implied that feeling. Then take turns sharing your responses in your small group, writing down on your worksheet the observations and inferences of others. The teacher should not comment until the group has finished. He then should share the situation and feeling specified on the card and his feelings while role-playing.
5. Each participant should have an opportunity to be "teacher."

Role-Playing

Situation: You and your spouse have had a silly argument. It was ridiculous to get so steamed up, but you still are. *Feeling*: fuming.

Situation: You and someone very close to you have just spent a very warm and tender hour together. *Feeling*: warmth.

WORKSHEET

ROLE-PLAYING FEELING COMMUNICATION

	Inferred feeling	Implicating behavior	Actual situation and feeling
Teacher 1	Me: Others:	Me: Others:	
Teacher 2	Me: Others:	Me: Others:	
Teacher 7	Me: Others:	Me: Others:	
Teacher 8	Me: Others:	Me: Others:	

Situation: You have just been told by your principal that your job has been eliminated due to budget concerns. He doesn't know if he'll be able to offer you another contract. *Feeling*: insecurity.

Situation: Your car broke down again on the way to school and you are late. *Feeling*: frustration.

Situation: You had a heated argument with someone in your car pool concerning his constant lateness. *Feeling*: hostility.

Situation: The film you planned to show this morning didn't arrive. *Feeling*: unpreparedness.

Situation: You have just found exactly the house you've always wanted at a price you can afford. *Feeling*: happiness.

Situation: It's the last day before spring vacation and tonight you are leaving for Bermuda. *Feeling*: carefree abandon.

Situation: You have a splitting headache. *Feeling*: physical discomfort, edginess.

Situation: You just found out that an important faculty meeting has been called for this afternoon. You already have plans to meet a friend at the airport at that time. *Feeling*: indecision.

Situation: The father of a student of yours has demanded a conference with you today. You have no idea why he wants to see you. *Feeling*: anxiety.

Situation: You have just learned that a teacher you are very fond of will not be rehired. *Feeling*: disappointment.

Situation: You have just won a $1,000 prize in a lottery drawing. *Feeling*: euphoria.

Situation: You have just learned that your most troublesome student is moving away. *Feeling*: relief.

Situation: You have just learned that you will be supervised by the principal today. *Feeling*: concern.

Situation: You didn't sleep well last night because of noise next door. *Feeling*: exhaustion.

Situation: The intramural team you are coaching won their game. *Feeling*: pride.

Situation: A student who has been troublesome talked at length with you, honestly and trustingly. *Feeling*: fulfillment.

Situation: Your suggestion for reorganizing your department was accepted, even though the department head, whom you dislike, disapproved. *Feeling*: smugness.

Questions

1. Were you comfortable trying to make your specified feeling explicit, or did you feel a need to try to hide the feeling? What do your responses indicate about the way you normally handle the expression of feeling?
2. As a teacher, do you usually—
   a. tell your students explicitly how you are feeling;
   b. convey how you are feeling, but without explicit words;
   c. try to ignore your underlying feelings;
   d. try to cover up all feelings and concentrate only on what is happening within the classroom;
   e. try to compensate for or cover up unpleasant feelings, but share pleasant ones.
3. What did you learn from your experience with this activity that you can use to make yourself a more effective teacher? How open do you *want* to be? What, specifically, can you do in the near future to make yourself more the way you would like to be?
4. Make a contract with yourself concerning something you can do with your communication of feeling to make yourself more effective. In two weeks review your contract, evaluate your achievement, and make a new self-contract.

Follow-up

Structured experiences in group situations become meaningful only when there is some carry-over into real life, when the observations you have made or the skills you have learned make an impact on the way you live. In a situation outside your small support group, observe the behavior of an individual and try to read the feelings that person may have brought into the situation from outside. You might observe anyone, but your observation will be most meaningful if you can share with and learn from the individual you observe. For example, you might work with another member of your support group: observe him in class, at a faculty meeting, or in a social situation, and afterward tell him what you observed and what you thought he was feeling. He can tell you what he actually was aware of feeling. Then the two of you can pursue whatever questions arise as a result of your exchange. Be sure to secure the cooperation of the person you observe if you plan to share your observation later. Also, if you are working with one other person, you might then exchange places and be observed.

Student Use

This activity can easily be varied for use with students of all ages. With early-elementary students, you might ask a child to show the feelings he would have if—

he just spent his only dime on a popsicle, and it falls off the stick into a mud puddle.
his best friend is going to spend the night with him.

An upper-elementary or junior-high student can show the feelings he would have if—

he and his older brother argue over what TV show to watch, and the brother wins.
he finally asked a girl he has liked for a long time to attend a party with him, and she has accepted.

A high-school student can show the feelings he would have if—

his parents have insisted that he stay home to baby-sit with his younger sister on Friday night, but all his friends are going to a movie.
his parents have just decided that they will help him buy a car.

SHADOWING

As a teacher, you have a responsibility to familiarize yourself with the school environment and the various functions in that school. Moreover, the greater your understanding of the other members of your school community, the greater your base from which to draw conclusions, make decisions, and facilitate resources. The ideal way to learn about the other members of your school would be to step into their shoes to find out what school life is like for them.

It is, of course, impossible to literally step into the shoes of another person and experience life exactly as he or she does. It is possible for each of us to develop empathy for the position in which another individual finds himself. One way to gather information is to read accounts of another's life (self-accounts or those gathered by others); another is through direct dialogue and discussion. While these methods are valuable, they are limited in that they cannot provide the depth and continuity that is necessary for a deep and complete empathetic relationship. In teaching, this kind of relationship is necessary, as it is in all helping professions.

Shadowing, often used by cultural anthropologists, is an activity that helps facilitate empathetic understanding at a high level by providing a means for gathering data about how another person sees and moves in his environment.

Objectives

1. To develop an empathetic understanding of different individuals in the school.
2. To discover data about different roles in the school and how individuals live in these roles.
3. To begin to use the data to make decisions, draw conclusions, and facilitate resources in teaching.

Directions

Select a person whose world you would like to learn more about: a student, a teacher, the principal, the school nurse—anyone who will give you permission to shadow him. Then, for at least one full day or smaller periods of time over more days, follow that person everywhere. Observe carefully how he reacts to the environment. Try to feel as that person seems to feel. Take whatever notes you think important concerning the way in which that individual experiences the school. In your journal, record discoveries and understandings that you make about the person you shadow, about the school, and about yourself.

Questions

1. What were the major problems or frustrations of your subject?
2. What were the major pleasures and joys of your subject?
3. How much of your subject's day, either directly or indirectly, has implications for your daily life at school?
4. In what matters can your shadow subject help your school life?
5. List some pointers for yourself in dealing with people who are in the position of your subject.

Follow-up

After you have shadowed at least two people, preferably more, you might wish to have someone you trust shadow you. Have the person shadow you for a substantial length of time. Afterward, sit down together and let the observer describe how he sees your role. Listen to his observations about how you function in that role. Feel free to ask him any questions about his report.

A second follow-up activity can be used in certain situations. If you know in advance that you must make a decision or present your ideas about an issue or interact with someone who must make a decision about you or that you will be involved in some appropriate situation, you might shadow the people involved to give you data for that upcoming event. For example, if you have thought of a plan to reduce stealing in the library that involves the custodian and the librarian, you might shadow these parties, after securing their permission, for short lengths of time. This will give you a better empathetic understanding of their responsibilities and attitudes.

Student Use

Shadowing is a significant learning instrument in the classroom. Use shadowing to help students gain insight and empathy for different members of the community. For example, the social-studies teacher might arrange for individual students to shadow various public servants—a mayor, city councilman, school superintendent, school-board member, police dispatcher, policeman, or postal clerk. Each student then reports to the class on the activities of the person shadowed. A math teacher might suggest that students shadow salesmen, cashiers, waitresses, bank officials, bank tellers, or loan officers. English teachers might suggest that students write short stories or characterizations based on persons they have shadowed.

KNOW YOUR STUDENTS

Even if over the years your teachers spend many hours with you, the chances are they won't know much about you. Your parents may know a bit more, and your friends will know most.

But you should realize that the school does have a lot of information about you. For example, the results of medical or psychological examinations, your exam results and teachers' reports. This information is treated as confidential, but it's available to teachers, police and child welfare authorities.

As a rule an ordinary teacher doesn't know what your living conditions are like;

where your father and mother work and how much they earn;

how many brothers and sisters you have and where they go to school;

how your parents get along together;

what your parents think of the teacher and the school;

what you do in your free time;

whether you like the teacher and the school;

whether you have a lot of interests outside school;

whether you have a paper route or another job;

how much time you spend on your homework.[7]

Every teacher we've known has wrestled with the question of how much he should know about his students. One popular view, upheld by many teachers, is that teachers cannot be fair if they know too much; therefore, teachers should not seek out information concerning their students' backgrounds, past performance, and experiences. According to this view, students can be treated fairly only if they are seen as equals, each with the same reservoir of untapped potential as all of his classmates. Thus these teachers avoid reading the students' cumulative folders and refrain from asking for or listening to the information and opinions of their colleagues who have known the students previously.

We recognize that the material in cumulative folders and the information and opinions of other teachers are often biased. We agree that many students have been unfairly judged and treated on the basis of incidents from the past. We strongly disagree, however, with the position that teachers should therefore avoid gathering information concerning their students. We believe it is impossible for teachers to work effectively with people they don't know.

It is imperative, of course, for teachers to be aware of the unique health problems of individual students and to treat each student accordingly. The child who is violently allergic to bee venom must be removed from a room containing a bee; the child with a serious heart murmur must be kept on the ground floor and away from strenuous exercise; the child with poor vision must be accommodated. No one argues that this physical information is not vital. We believe that information concerning the child's psychological, social, familial, and economic world is also

---

[7] Søren Hansen and Jesper Jensen, *The Little Red Schoolbook*, trans. Berit Thornberry (New York: Pocket Books, a division of Simon & Schuster, Inc., 1971), pp. 55–56. Copyright © 1971 by stage 1, London.

vital. The child who is a member of a large, closely knit extended family lives in a different world from the only child who lives with his widowed mother, and each must be accepted and responded to accordingly. Just as children are not identical physically, they are not identical emotionally, socially, or in any other way, and should not be considered as if they were. The fair teacher reaches out and responds to children according to their unique histories, circumstances, and needs.

Objectives

1. To be aware of the unique histories, circumstances, and needs of your students.
2. To use constructively the information you have in order to respond individually and appropriately to each child.

Directions

Select questions from the list below and add other appropriate questions in order to make up a questionnaire for your students to complete. With young children, you might choose to ask a few questions at many different times. With older students, you can use one comprehensive questionnaire, or you can group the questions dealing with similar issues and distribute brief response sheets (five questions or less) regularly. If you choose the latter method, you will probably discover from reading students' responses many more important questions that you can include on subsequent sheets. For the information to be useful, of course, students must identify themselves. Remember that they must also have the right *not* to respond and should be assured that they may choose not to answer any question or questions.

1. How old are you? What is good about being the age you are?
2. Name at least one important hobby or interest of yours. How much time do you give this activity each week?
3. What is your ethnic heritage (race and nationality of your parents and grandparents)? How important to your family is this heritage?
4. Where do you live? Is it a house, apartment, mobile home? How long have you lived there? (*Teacher:* drive through your students' neighborhoods—or better yet, walk—noting where they live.)
5. With whom do you live? With whom do you share a bedroom? Where is your favorite spot at home?
6. What do your parents do for a living?
7. How do you usually spend your afterschool hours?

8. With whom do you eat lunch?

9. Who are your three best friends? Write a little bit about each.

10. What responsibilities do you have at home? How do you feel about them?

11. Name one thing you do very well.

12. What are your favorite foods? TV shows? colors? academic subjects?

13. What is your astrological sign? Does it mean anything to you?

14. How much spending money do you have each week? Where do you get it? How do you spend it?

15. What is your major ambition for the next year?

16. What occupational plans have you made for your future?

17. What embarrasses you?

18. Who, if anyone, helps you with homework?

19. What adult are you closest to? Describe this person briefly.

20. Do you consider yourself a leader or a follower? Why?

21. What books have you read in the last month? Which had something important to say to you?

22. What magazines or newspapers do you read regularly?

23. How did you spend the last two Saturday afternoons?

24. If you could go anywhere in the world tomorrow, where would you go?

Follow-up

You might use some of the questions from the list above as small-group discussion topics with your students. Any question could easily serve to motivate open and honest communication among students. The emphasis at any one time is on a single communication skill—listening, giving positive feedback, self-disclosure, or reflection.

LOG CONVERSATION: WHO LEARNS WHAT WHERE?

Rick: I've noticed that many authors are saying that teachers generally don't teach what they think they're teaching. According to Ivan Illich,

Orphans, idiots, and schoolteachers' sons learn most of what they learn outside the "educational" process planned for them. Teachers have made a poor showing in their attempts at increasing learning among the poor. Poor parents who want their children to go to school are less concerned about what they will learn than about the certificate and money they will earn. And middle-class parents commit their children to a teacher's care to keep them from learning what the poor learn on the streets. Increasingly educational research demonstrates that children learn most of what teachers pretend to teach them from peer groups, from comics, from chance observations, and above all from mere participation in the ritual of school. Teachers, more often than not, obstruct such learning of subject matters as goes on in school.[8]

As I think back, I recall that my most significant learning occurred outside of school. For example, the best lesson I ever had in human relations came while driving a cab in Boston. I learned how to work with fractions while playing a baseball game with dice. Where did you readers learn some of the important things you now know?

You:

Barbara: When I try to remember what I learned from specific elementary and secondary teachers that I had, I remember things that had nothing to do with the subject matter involved. For example, my third-grade teacher taught me that it was more important to raise my hand and wait to be called on than to have good answers. What specific learning do you readers recall that came from specific elementary and secondary teachers that you had?

You:

INCIDENTAL LEARNINGS

A classroom can be compared to a communications system, for certainly there is a flow of messages between teacher (transmitter) and pupils (receivers) and among the pupils; contacts are made and broken, messages can be sent at a certain rate of speed only, and so on. But there is also another interesting characteristic of communications systems that is applicable to classrooms, and that is their inherent tendency to generate *noise*. *Noise,* in communications theory, applies to all those fluctuations of the system that cannot be controlled. They are the sounds that are not part of the message.[9]

[8] Ivan Illich, *Deschooling Society* (New York: Harper & Row, 1971), p. 29.
[9] Jules Henry, *Culture Against Man* (New York: Random House, 1963), p. 289.

The noise of the classroom generates learning among the students that is incidental to the message or subject matter itself. Incidental learnings are those that the students learn outside of the curriculum planned by the teacher. Students are continually learning from the classroom and from you much that you are not even aware of. Imagine a teacher who continually tells students that his purpose as a teacher is to encourage individual thought and creativity, yet in class he responds positively only when students offer "right" answers he has already decided upon and tries to elicit, word for word, from students. Instead of the verbal message encouraging independent and creative thought, students quickly learn that in this class only the thinking that conforms exactly to the teacher's thinking is rewarded. They learn not to answer unless they know what the teacher is thinking.

The arrangement of the classroom itself teaches all who see it something about the person who arranged it, probably the teacher. A teacher who talks about the importance of students interacting with and teaching one another belies her statement if her room is arranged with rows of students' desks facing her desk in the front of the room. She may *say* that student interaction is vital, but she teaches that all interaction should be with her.

Objectives

1. To understand the concept of incidental learnings.
2. To recognize possible incidental learnings from the behavior of others.
3. To develop an awareness of the incidental learnings you may be passing on to your students.

Directions

On the worksheet included are some examples of patterns likely to foster incidental learnings. Imagine yourself a student in the class in which each example is practiced. What consequences do you imagine would result from each of the incidental learnings described?

As you observe classes, try to note probable incidental learnings in that environment and keep a list in your journal.

Questions

1. Which of the patterns of teacher behavior described above have you seen in classrooms you have observed?

As a student in the class of each of the following teachers, what might you learn from the behavior of the teacher? How would you most likely respond?

Teacher 1: Seems to have secrets that students are expected to guess.
Examples of teacher talk:

"What do you think we're going to do today?"

"I'm thinking of a word. Can anyone tell me what the word is? It starts with 'E.' "

"You'd better pay attention, because this is important and just might be on the test."

I would learn _____

I would respond _____

Teacher 2: Student's answer is never sufficient. Teacher repeats it verbatim for the rest of the class or elaborates on it.

I would learn _____

I would respond _____

Teacher 3: Asks only questions that have short, specific answers.
Examples of teacher talk:

"America was discovered by?"

"Three and what are seven?"

"Was Socrates a real person?"

I would learn _____

I would respond _____

Teacher 4: Responds to almost every pupil's recitation with a stereotyped "OK, very good."

I would learn _____

I would respond _____

Teacher 5: Gives assignments to be done at home but never again refers to the material in any way.

I would learn _____

I would respond _____

Teacher 6: Seems rewarded by seeing a sea of waving hands and often asks poll-taking questions.
Examples of teacher talk:

"How many of you read the chapter?"

"How many of you understood this?"

"I don't see many hands!"

I would learn _____

I would respond _____

Teacher 7: Begins nearly every utterance with the phrase "Who would like to. . ?" The same phrase is used to ask content questions and to get someone to wash the chalkboard.

I would learn _____

I would respond _____

Teacher 8: Frequently (if not always) phrases questions as if students were doing her a personal favor by answering.
Examples of teacher talk:

"Who can *tell me* who discovered America?"

"Who would like to read the next page *for me?*"

"Who can *give me* the answer to number four?"

"Sally, put your answer on the board *for me,* please."

I would learn _____

I would respond _____

Teacher 9: Asks questions that facilitate the giving of opinions and free interchange.

I would learn _____

I would respond _____

Teacher 10: Often redirects questions asked of her to other students.
Examples of teacher talk:

"I'm not certain, Joe, but perhaps someone else has an idea?"

"That's an interesting question, Marge. Can anyone help us out?"

I would learn _____

I would respond _____

2. Which may be present in your classroom?
3. What other incidental learnings do you imagine might be present in your classroom?

LOG CONVERSATION: ANONYMOUS PERSON

Barbara: Yesterday while visiting a fourth-grade classroom, I couldn't help but notice an extremely disruptive student who succeeded in commanding about ninety percent of the teacher's time. He frustrated both her and the other students. It made me think of something that Rollo May said in *Love and Will*. Last night I looked it up again.

The mood of the anonymous person is, If I cannot affect or touch anybody, I can at least shock you into some feeling, force you into some passion through wounds and pain; I shall at least make sure we both feel something, and I shall force you to see me and know that I am also here! Many a child or adolescent has forced the group to take cognizance of him by destructive behavior, and though he is condemned, at least the community notices him. To be actively hated is almost as good as being actively liked; it breaks down the utterly unbearable situation of anonymity and aloneness.[10]

Can you readers describe any students you have now that fit the description above?

You:

Rick: What suppressive techniques have you readers seen used to deal with this type of student? What positive ways can you think of to deal with him?

You:

Barbara: Making contact with people around me is very important to me. Do you readers feel that you make enough contact? Do you

[10] Rollo May, *Love and Will* (New York: W. W. Norton, 1969), p. 31. Copyright © 1969 by W. W. Norton & Company, Inc.

touch others in some way often enough each day? What can you do to increase your contacts?

You:

POSITIVE STUDENT-CONFRONTATION

In relating with our students, we must be careful not to permit small irritations to accumulate under our skin, where they build into resentments and become potential sources of hostility. Feelings of hostility can have a powerful negative effect on relations with individuals and classes as a whole. To prevent a stockpiling of resentments, it is helpful to deal with the irritating incidents as they occur by sharing our feelings with the students who are causing us the irritation.

In actual classroom situations it very often seems difficult to deal with problems openly and positively. The pressures of the situation and the presence of the other students sometimes seem to mitigate against dealing spontaneously with feelings. We are also tempted either to ignore the situations and let resentments slowly build into potential hostility or to attack the students by putting them down in some way. While either of these practices might alleviate the situation for a time, they usually do little to solve the problem in the long run. Positive student-confrontation, however, can lead to open communication between you and your students so that negotiation and compromise can be used to solve relationship conflicts.

Confronting students positively takes practice because for most of us it is an unfamiliar behavior. The following activity is to be used for practice so that you develop the necessary skills before transferring them to your classroom.

Objectives

1. To understand the nature of positive student-confrontation.
2. To use positive student-confrontation effectively.

Directions

To practice student confrontation you need a group of six or more people, preferably about ten. One person volunteers to be "teacher," one person volunteers to be "coach," and the rest are "students." Each member of the group should have a chance to be teacher, coach, and student in successive rounds. The teacher separates from the students and prepares a ten-minute lesson in any subject for an appropriate age group. The students, meanwhile, plan to role-play different "student types." The types can include a bored student, a troublemaker, an arrogant student, a brown-nose, any type of student that might be found in a classroom. (In role-playing students, it is helpful not to get so locked into the role that you do not react normally to stimuli from the teacher or other students. The quiet student, for example, should speak if he has something to say. The troublemaker should behave if the teacher effectively does something to cause him to settle down.) The coach at this time need not prepare anything.

When everyone is ready, the teacher begins the lesson with the students role-playing at the age suggested by the teacher. The students slightly exaggerate their roles to make the experience more enriching. The coach is an observer at this time. Once the lesson is completed, the teacher chooses one student who made him the most uncomfortable. The two, teacher and student, sit face to face and engage in positive confrontation as described below. Now the coach plays the important role of keeping the confrontation positive by not allowing destructive statements (personal attacks), by keeping the participants on the subject, and by making sure that each participant has an equal opportunity to speak.

The Confrontation

The teacher states what he resented in the student by using a sentence similar to the following: "When you . . . , I resented it because . . ." The student responds by stating a resentment to the teacher using a similar sentence. Both resentments must be stated clearly so that teacher and student understand exactly what the other means. In sharing feelings, avoid placing blame or guilt on the student, for this only creates defensiveness and blocks open communication. Statements that begin with "I feel . . ." or "When you . . . , I feel . . ." often are the most constructive. To assure understanding, the student should restate the teacher's resentment to the satisfaction of the teacher, and the teacher should restate the student's resentment to the satisfaction of the student.

Next the teacher makes a demand on the student; the student responds with a demand on the teacher. Once the demands are clearly stated and restated, the two participants negotiate until both have decided to do something with which they are both comfortable that will remove or reduce the cause for resentment. Repeat the process as many times as necessary to deal with all the resentments between the teacher and student. The following examples of positive student-confrontation will clarify the process.

Example One is taken from a student confrontation activity with college students role-playing a high-school teacher and students.

STATED RESENTMENTS

Teacher: I resented it when you talked to the boy next to you because I felt that you didn't care what I was saying.

Student: I resented it when you kept asking me to turn around and pay attention. It embarrassed me and made me feel small.

Coach: Do you both understand what the other has said?

Teacher and Student: Yes.

RESTATED RESENTMENTS

Student: You felt that when I was talking to the boy next to me, that I wasn't listening to what you were saying.

Teacher: You didn't like it when I kept asking you to turn around and pay attention, because it embarrassed you.

Coach: Okay, go on.

DEMANDS

Teacher: I demand that you pay attention to me when I am lecturing.

Student: I demand that you let me talk to my friend when I am bored with your lecture.

NEGOTIATION AND RESOLUTION

Teacher: I can't let you talk to your friends during my lecture because it will disturb others. Besides, the information might be important to the unit.

Student: I can see that it will disturb others, but why should I have to pay attention if I already know the material? I demand that you let me pass notes to my friend if I know the material. That way I won't disturb anyone.

Teacher: I think passing notes will still cause a disturbance, but I can see that you will be bored if you are already familiar with the material. I can let you know just before class what the lecture will be about. If you feel you are familiar enough with it, you can go to the library. You can keep this privilege as long as you maintain your present academic level.

Student: That sounds good. And if I do elect to stay in your class, I won't pass notes or talk to my friend.

Coach: Are you both satisfied with this resolution?

Student and Teacher: Yes.

Coach: Each of you restate your solutions.

RESTATED RESOLUTION

Student: You said that passing notes would cause a disturbance, but that I may go to the library if I feel that I would be bored during the lesson because I may be familiar with the material already.

Teacher: You said that you'd like that arrangement and that if you decide to stay in the class, you won't pass notes or talk to your friend.

Notice in this example that neither the student nor the teacher attacked the other. Both maintained a high level of honesty and openness. Each considered the other's demand and reacted to it as a real possibility. In the end they reached a compromised solution that was comfortable for each of them, a solution that might never have been considered without the confrontation.

In *Example Two* college students are role-playing fifth-graders.

RESENTMENTS

Teacher: I resented it when you kept throwing your reading book on the floor because it was very frustrating to me. I took it as a personal insult.

Student: I resented it when you told me I had to read the same book as yesterday because I already finished it. It makes me think you don't care how well I read.

Teacher: Well, you didn't have to keep throwing it on the floor. It was really aggravating.

RESTATEMENTS

Coach: Careful not to blame the student. Restate each other's resentments.

Teacher: You resent having to read the same thing over again just because the rest of the class hasn't finished as much as you have.

Student: That's right. And you resent my throwing the book down.

Teacher: Correct.

Coach: OK, now state your demands.

DEMANDS

Teacher: I demand that you don't throw your book on the floor.

Student: I demand that you let me read ahead if I am ahead of my reading group.

NEGOTIATION AND RESOLUTION

Teacher: I don't mind if you read ahead, but how can I help you if you leave the reading group? I have no way to hear you read and see how well you are doing.

Student: I get frustrated when I have to read out loud what I have already read to myself. It's the most boring thing in the world to wait for the other students.

Teacher: Would you be willing to give up some of your free time to read to me so that I will be able to see how well you are reading?

Student: Uh, well, OK. I'll give up some of my free studytime to read to you.

Teacher: I have an idea. If you read well, then during the group-reading session, you can work with one of the other readers. That will help me and give you something constructive to do.

Student: OK, but I can read what books I want for my own reading.

Teacher: That's OK with me.

These examples are of college students role-playing student and teacher. Real dialogue in a classroom does not usually develop so perfectly along the model of positive student-confrontation. However, by meeting with students after school and giving them a brief explanation of the rules of positive student-confrontation, you can achieve very positive results. Also, a teacher can have small confrontations while the class is actually in session.

Teacher: Elliot, it's very difficult to talk to the class when you throw spitballs. I would like you to stop.

Elliot: I'm sorry.

Teacher: Is there anything *I* can do to help you stop throwing them?

Questions

1. What did you learn about yourself in the role of teacher?
2. What did you learn about yourself in the role of student?
3. What difficulties did you encounter in positive confrontation?

4. What did you learn about the person you confronted?

5. How can you best use positive student-confrontation with your students?

Follow-up

Once you have mastered the techniques of positive student-confrontation, you may develop a personal style for classroom use. When you feel that you are ready, make a list of as many specific resentments that you feel in your classes as possible. Rank the completed list, numbering the most important *1,* the second most important *2,* and so on. After each resentment place a demand that you can make on your class or student to remove or reduce the cause of that resentment. Start with the top of your list and try to resolve your problem by working a compromise with your students. Make your demand in a positive way and ask for a demand in return.

JOB APPLICATION

Each of us is faced daily with situations that call upon us to evaluate our effectiveness, our goals, our assets and our liabilities. We seldom take the time, however, to appraise ourselves specifically and thoroughly and to put that appraisal into writing (for personal use only). A fictitious job application, which you must complete twice—once by honestly appraising yourself and once as you actually would complete a real application—

School of the Future
U.S.A.

Answer honestly the questions below. This form is private. You need not share your responses with anyone.

1. For what position are you applying? Why this position?

_____

_____

_____

2. What have you done in the past two years that prepared you for it?

_____

_____

_____

3. What are your most favorable characteristics for this particular position?

_____

_____

_____

4. What liabilities will you have in this position?

_____

_____

_____

5. Will you still want this position in five years? Explain.

_____

_____

_____

6. Why should we hire you?

_____

_____

_____

7. Name three references to whom we can write.

_____

_____

_____

Answer the questions below as if you were completing an actual job application. Sell yourself to the prospective employer.

1. For what position are you applying? Why this position?

_____

_____

_____

2. What have you done in the past two years that prepared you for it?

_____

_____

_____

3. What are your most favorable characteristics for this particular position?

_____

_____

_____

4. What liabilities will you have in this position?

_____

_____

_____

5. Will you still want this position in five years? Explain.

_____

_____

_____

6. Why should we hire you?

_____

_____

_____

7. Name three references to whom we can write.

_____

_____

_____

lets you privately assess your purposes, strengths, and weaknesses as a teacher.

Objectives

1. To openly assess your goals, assets, and liabilities as a teacher.
2. To compare your honest self-evaluation with your self-presentation to a prospective employer.

Directions

Imagine that you are applying for a teaching job. You are asked to answer the questions on Worksheet 1. The only difference between the worksheet and a real application is that you are trying not to sell yourself, but to look honestly at yourself. Complete Worksheet 1.

When you have finished, look over your answers. Check those you would answer differently on an actual application. Then turn to Worksheet 2, and complete the application as if you were actually going to submit it for consideration for a position you very much want.

Questions

1. In question seven on both worksheets you named three references. Why did you choose each of the three? Would you still choose the same three if you knew they would be totally honest in their evaluations of you?
2. Did you have difficulty answering any question honestly? What do you think caused the difficulty?
3. Which questions did you respond to differently on the two applications? What does this difference in response mean to you?
4. Read over your responses on both forms. If you were the hiring official for the position, would you hire someone who submitted an application like yours? Have you assessed yourself honestly?

Follow-up

If you are working closely with a small support group, you might use your group to review each other's applications. You can review either those completed as actual applications or those done as honest self-evaluations. Prepare copies of the applications for one another. Then each of you can present your application in turn, perhaps enlarging upon them. Ask for honest feedback from the others about how they see you as a teacher. Your group can also act as a personnel committee, reviewing each of the applications and commenting on how the candidate might function in your school. (This can be a somewhat threatening activity. It should be used only if all of you feel trusting and comfortable with one another.) Naturally, any individual has the right not to participate, and that decision must be unquestionably accepted by the others.

Student Use

Your students, like all of us, probably love to talk and write about themselves, which facilitates the use of the job application in the classroom. Youngsters of junior-high-school age and older might be asked to write want ads for the classified section of an imaginary newspaper, selling their services in some capacity. For example, a young girl might write something like the following:

> For hire: thirteen-year-old female to design and make handcrafted macramé belts; have been working with macramé for two years; able to create original designs to meet your specifications. Intelligent, careful, talented, able to work fast and under pressure. See Sally Matthews for samples and estimates.

These ads can then be displayed on a bulletin board or collected and printed up in a Class Classified newsheet.

High-school students might also be interested in completing job applications, either those on the accompanying worksheets or actual job applications collected from agencies, businesses, and industries. Thus they can learn some important procedures concerning job applications while examining themselves as potential job applicants.

LOG CONVERSATION: YEAR OFF

Barbara: You know, I had the best year of teaching I ever had after coming back to it from a couple years' experience in the business world. I wonder if it wouldn't be a good idea for all teachers to get away from teaching for a while.

Rick: Postman and Weingartner say just that in *Teaching As a Subversive Activity,* as does *The Little Red Schoolbook*:

> Things should be arranged so that each teacher, every now and then, automatically gets a year off so that he can get experience in something apart from teaching, instead of getting stale and out of touch with the world outside school. At the moment, if a teacher ever does get a year

free he usually has to go back to "school," yet again, and sit and learn from more books. Much of his knowledge won't be of any use to you, but he won't get a chance to find out about many things which would be useful to you.[11]

I wonder if any of you readers have had or know of instances where a teacher took a year or two off. What were the results?

You:

Rick: I sometimes fantasize things I would like to do with a year off, like assisting a professional photographer or racing motorcycles. What do you readers fantasize as possible growth-oriented activities that you could pursue, outside of education, with a year off?

You:

TEACHER-EDUCATION PROGRAM

As teachers and prospective teachers, all of us have been involved in one way or another with teacher education. We have developed some opinions about teacher education. Based on the experiences you have had, what do you think is essential for a teacher?

By filling in the accompanying worksheet, you will outline the knowledge, competencies, practical experiences, and exposure to issues that you would include in an ideal teacher-education program. Use the space at the bottom of the worksheet to include anything we have overlooked. In each category list two or three specific recommendations. Obviously, your outline can only be suggestive of your major areas of concern. Do not try to outline a comprehensive or exhaustive program.

When you have identified specific bits of knowledge, competencies, experiences, and issues that are important to you, you may want to share your findings with others. In your support group compare your individual responses to the worksheet. As you listen to the responses that others

[11] Hansen and Jensen, *The Little Red Schoolbook*, p. 50.

To be an effective teacher, a person needs:

KNOWLEDGE

    essential:

    recommended:

    optional:

COMPETENCIES

    essential:

    recommended:

    optional:

PRACTICAL EXPERIENCES

    essential:

    recommended:

    optional:

EXPOSURE TO IDEAS

    essential:

    recommended:

    optional:

OTHER

1. To be a good teacher, a person should know—

2. To be a good teacher, a person should be able to—

3. To be a good teacher, a person should be—

made, indicate on your worksheet those you accept as important and those you question by adding them in the appropriate places. Try to understand the thinking of your colleagues in their responses.

You might collaborate on designing one program that you all agree on. You then might assist one another in obtaining the components of the program that each of you consider necessary for yourself. Use each other; perhaps an experience you consider necessary (but have not yet experienced) is available in a colleague's classroom. Perhaps you are quite well-versed in an area of knowledge to which a colleague wants exposure. For example, perhaps your colleague can provide you with an experience with a handicapped child, and you may be able to teach her how to conduct a brainstorming session. Every small group has a wealth of available resources. Take the time to discover and use them.

Student Use

The Ideal Teacher-Training Program worksheet can also be used to collect information from your students. Those of adolescent age can respond to the worksheet as it is with their ideas about the knowledge, competencies, experiences, and issues that they would like teachers to have and express. Younger students can use Worksheet 2 or a similar one. You will undoubtedly find a great deal of valuable information . . . and perhaps a few surprises.

3

Examining
Your Teaching Self

The activities in chapter two were internally focused. They were designed to help you look inward at your emotions, values, goals, attitudes, beliefs, and past behavior. The activities in this chapter are externally focused. They will help you collect valuable data about observable phenomena in the classroom—your classroom and any others that you may observe. What you do with that data is then up to you.

The classroom can be viewed as a huge game of chess with each of its numerous parts functioning in an interdependent relationship with all the rest. When you look at the whole, you see only seemingly meaningless and undirected activity. When you understand how each apparently independent movement affects the others, then you begin to understand the complex interdependence of the whole. The activities in this chapter are designed to help you recognize the many individual classroom functions and behaviors that so vitally affect the complex whole. As in learning to play chess, you must focus on single, manageable movements before you can analyze and effectively manipulate the total environment.

The first stage in examining your teaching self is data collection. Interpretation, evaluation, and judgment have no place in data collection.

As a data collector, you are simply gathering information. Be careful not to preselect outcomes, not to let your biases influence the data you collect, and to avoid interpretation while collecting data. Continually keep in mind the absolute necessity of remaining as open and objective as possible (realizing, of course, that complete objectivity is humanly impossible). You are only a recorder at this stage. Interpretation and evaluation come only after collection.

In some cases you will be receiving data collected about you and your classroom. As a receiver, remember that the data you receive is non-evaluative, so you do not have to defend it. Accept the data as one individual's observations. Once you have the data, you will use it to check for congruence between your ideal teaching self and you as you act in the classroom. With the data you will generate alternatives and will experiment with new behavior of your choosing.

All the activities in this chapter provide means for gathering and examining data. Adapt these methods in any way that is appropriate for you: use student data-collectors, audio-tapes and video-tapes, and new designs that occur to you as you go through any of the processes. All the methods are flexible enough to accommodate individual needs. All will provide you with concrete material to increase your awareness of that excitingly complex environment we call a classroom.

REACTION SHEETS

As teachers we experience daily a myriad of emotions, reactions, and impressions. These come in such rapid succession that often we are unable to sort them out, think them through, and make any sense of them. Yet they all influence us in one way or another, and therefore deserve to be brought as fully into our awareness as possible.

Some people process their experiences by keeping extensive diaries. No doubt they find such diary-writing to be a highly significant and rewarding experience. They focus on the most important aspects of their daily lives and keep a running record of their significant concerns, a record that is always available to them for examination and review. Many of us, however, have difficulty letting the words flow, or we don't make the time, or we simply don't enjoy writing extensively. Yet we too could profit from the experience of recording the significant impressions, feelings, and attitudes of our lives; we too could thereby increase our awareness of the most meaningful influences on our lives. We think it is vitally and especially important for teachers to be aware of what influences us, for we in turn influence our students. Daily and weekly reaction sheets, kept as part of our journals, provide a quick, simple, yet meaningful way to keep track of all that influences our lives significantly.

Objectives

1. To consistently record significant influences in your life.
2. To analyze those influences on your life that cause you to respond in particular ways.

Directions

Daily reaction sheets. Each day complete a daily reaction sheet like the one on the accompanying Worksheet 1. Date your data sheet and note your major teaching responsibilities for the day. Before your first class and after your last class complete a "Here and Now" (see "There and Then," p. 24). In each of the four quadrants write a word or short phrase that describes a feeling you are experiencing at the moment. You may use both physical and emotional feelings—for example, you may be feeling *exhausted* and *warm* and *contented* and *friendly*. Then, next to the circle, expand upon the most dominant feeling in a sentence or two. When you complete the second "Here and Now" after your last class, also note the high point and the low point of your day, the experiences that comprised the best and the worst parts of your day.

Weekly reaction sheets. Every Friday afternoon, just after the week's teaching responsibilities have ended, complete the accompanying Worksheet 2.

Questions

The worth of daily or weekly reaction sheets lies not in the individual sheet, but in the patterns they reveal over a period of time. At the end of a week, two weeks, or a month, arrange your daily reaction sheets before you. Do the same with your weekly reaction sheets after a month or six weeks. You might then structure the analysis of your reaction sheets around the following questions:

1. Do you see any patterns in your responses to particular portions of the sheets? What do these patterns mean to you?
2. What incidents provide consistent high points and consistent low

Date: _____　　　Responsibilities: _____

Time: _____　　　Strongest feeling: _____

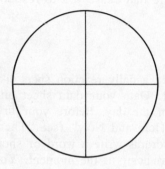

Time: _____　　　Strongest feeling: _____

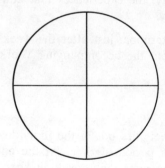

The high point of the day was —

The low point of the day was —

Date:

1. What was your biggest project of the past week? Comment on its success.

2. What were the high and low points of the week?

3. Who was your most rewarding student during the past week? Why?

4. Who was your most troublesome student during the past week? Why?

5. Describe your relationship with each of the aforementioned students.

6. Explain one thing you did this past week that you would do differently if you had it to do again.

7. Finish the sentence: "This week in the classroom for me was—"

8. Open comment on the week:

points? What function do high points and low points serve in your life? What can you do to provide yourself with the right number and kind of high points for you?

3. What constitutes success in your view, as revealed by your worksheets? How can you influence the amount of success you experience?
4. What do your worksheets tell you about your life as a teacher?
5. Are any changes indicated for you? How can you effect them?
6. Do your high points indicate that you are satisfied with your job? If not, what changes are indicated?

Student Use

Students, too, can look over their days and weeks and record how it went for them. The daily reaction sheet can be used as is for students. After a significant number of days (perhaps fourteen to twenty-one days) the students can look for patterns in their lives and areas of concern. They can then determine possible changes that they might make.

The weekly reaction sheet would have to be modified to pertain to the events of a student's, rather than a teacher's, week. Some questions for such a sheet are:

1. What was your biggest project of the past week? Comment on it.
2. What were the high and low points of the week?
3. Who was your most rewarding friend (or relative) during the past week?
4. Who was your most troublesome friend (or relative) during the past week?
5. Describe your relationship with each of the people mentioned above.
6. Describe one thing you did this past week that you might do differently another time.
7. This week life for me was—
8. Open comment on the week:

INTERVIEWS

A school has many different people with many divergent perceptions and opinions concerning life in that school. A school is also affected by physical considerations, finance, administrative procedures, local politics, parental involvement, and a whole host of other influences. As a teacher or prospective teacher, you can function best if you know as much as possible about the school you are in. Unless you are aware of the practices, concerns, influences, and attitudes that exist in your school, you will be unable to know the ones that are important and influence the way you conduct yourself and your classroom.

Objectives

1. To be aware of the practices, influences, concerns, and attitudes that comprise your school.
2. To compare various individuals' perceptions of life in your school.
3. To collect data for determining your behavior in your school.

Directions

Many of the facts and procedures of your school are probably public knowledge, and you need to be aware of them. Other matters are in the realm of opinion. The student-council president, for example, may have a very different view of the principal than the youngster who constitutes the school's greatest behavior problem. Interviewing students, teachers, administrators, janitors, cooks, librarians, board members, parents, and anyone else with interest in the school can provide you with a wealth of data about life in its environment. Consider yourself an anthropologist visiting this unique culture for the first time.

The following questions require answers that will help you understand your school's ever-changing environment. In addition, ask students about the school: what they like and dislike, how they spend their days, where their favorite spots in school are, what the best time of day is, how the food in the cafeteria is (compare with the cook's answer), and what makes good teachers.

Interview Questions

BUILDINGS AND GROUNDS

1. When was the school built? For how many students? How many now attend?
2. What educational philosophy does the architecture of the building reveal? Is that philosophy still accepted and practiced?
3. What recreational facilities are provided? Who may use them? When may they be used?

4. Do the buildings and grounds adequately serve the needs of the students? of the community?
5. Who is responsible for maintenance? With what problems does the maintenance crew have to contend?

STAFF

1. List all nonteaching staff members, with a brief description of the responsibilities of each (secretaries, cooks, etc.).
2. Ask each of the nonteaching staff the following questions:
   a. What is the purpose of the school?
   b. What is the school's biggest problem?
   c. In what area does the school do its best job?
   d. What change or changes would you encourage or support?

FACULTY

1. How many full-time faculty members are there? How many part-time?
2. What is the proportion of men to women on the faculty? Are either men or women concentrated in one or a few grade levels or subject areas?
3. What proportion of the faculty have advanced degrees? What proportion are first-year teachers? What proportion have between one and five years' experience? between five and ten years' experience? over ten years' experience?
4. How closely do the cultural characteristics of the faculty reflect those of the community?
5. Is the faculty associated with a professional association, a union, or both? What proportion of the faculty belong to each? Who is the school representative to each organization? What differences and similarities exist between professional organizations?

PARENTS

1. Does the school have a parent or parent-teacher organization? If so, who are the officers? Ask each of them the following questions:
   a. What is the purpose of the organization?
   b. What is the best thing the organization has done in the last year?
   c. What proportion of the parents belong? What proportion are active?
   d. What changes would you encourage or support?

2. Do parents visit the school frequently? Do they contribute to the program? Are they formally invited and encouraged to take part?

GENERAL INFORMATION

1. What are the geographical boundaries of the school?
2. Describe the social, economic, and cultural characteristics of the school population.
3. How does the school respond to the unique social, economic, and cultural characteristics of the school population?
4. What overt or subtle cultural conflicts exist in the school? How do teachers and administrators respond to them?

SOCIAL POLICIES

1. Does the school have a written philosophy? If so, read it. Who wrote it? When? How closely do actual practices reflect the written philosophy and policy?
2. Describe detention, suspension, and expulsion policies. For what offenses can a student be detained, suspended, or expelled? Are all students treated equally under the policy?
3. What procedures must be followed regarding tardiness, absenteeism, truancy, early dismissal, recess, and lunchtime?
4. How are the outstanding achievements of certain students recognized?
5. What are the grading or evaluation policies and procedures?
6. What procedures exist in the library? the health room? the counseling office?
7. To whom does a teacher send a student for disciplinary reasons?
8. Are student rights clearly defined? Are students in this school denied any rights that the U.S. Constitution guarantees? If so, what?

STUDENT LIFE

1. Is there a student government? How is it organized? What function does it serve? How are students selected? How involved are students in school issues?
2. What extracurricular activities exist for students? How popular are they?
3. Have the students formed cliques? Describe each.
4. How do students dress? Who determines how they dress?
5. List the three major interests of students, as you see them.

Student Use

In the same way that you have just examined practices, procedures, and viewpoints in your school, so too might students of all ages examine their environments. Young children might ask questions about school practices or about procedures in a supermarket, police station, fire station, or another place of interest that you might visit. Older students might ask about school practices or about procedures in court (juvenile, traffic, criminal), various social agencies (welfare department, city school-administration), business, or in another area of interest. Students might ask such questions as these:

Who would I have to see if I wanted a job in a supermarket?

What hours does a fireman work?

If I get a traffic ticket, what procedure do I follow to plead "not guilty"?

For which traffic offenses might I have to appear in court?

If you are going to ask students to find the answers to important questions, it will be most advantageous for *them* to select the areas they wish to investigate and generate a list of questions. These lists might best be generated in group-brainstorming sessions (see "Brainstorming," pp. 14–15), in which students are encouraged to share in a supportive environment whatever may be on their minds. An order and coherence can be drawn and a list compiled from all the generated material. Students can then be sent off to find the answers to their questions.

SELF-ASSESSMENT SENTENCE STEMS

Self-assessment sentence stems are open-ended sentence beginnings that require us to consider our thoughts, feelings, and actions in teaching. If done on a regular basis, the sentence stems generate a collection of data that will help us inventory our patterns (similar to the reaction sheets, p. 106, and "How Did It Go?", p. 187). By becoming aware of our patterns, we are better able to identify those areas of our teaching we consider positive, those areas we may wish to modify slightly, and those areas we may wish to change more drastically. The analysis of our sentence-stem completions makes it possible for us to take the first steps in self-improvement.

Objectives

1. To gather data over a significant period of time concerning your thoughts, feelings, and actions in teaching.
2. To discover areas in your teaching that call for change.
3. To begin to take the steps necessary for making the indicated changes.

Directions

Complete the sentence stems on the accompanying Worksheets 1 and 2, leaving out any that are inappropriate for you. Try not to talk around the subject with drawn-out answers: be concise and to the point.
For example, rather than saying:

I feel bad when I haven't taken all the steps necessary for having my lesson ready by the time when I have to teach it.

Say:

I feel bad when I'm not prepared.

Once you have completed the sentence stems, code them in the manner suggested below. No response should have more than one code. Try to select the most appropriate code for each sentence. Each code may be used any number of times. Some sentences may not have a code.

Codings

Place *P* next to those sentences that make you *proud.*

Place *C* next to those sentences that make you feel *comfortable.*

Place *UN* next to those sentences that make you feel *uncomfortable.*

Place *ME* next to those sentences that you feel you have *control over.*

Place *NO* next to those sentences that you feel you have *no control over.*

Place *D* next to those sentences that you *wish were different.*

You may wish to modify or change the above coding system. You must use the codes that are most appropriate for you. Other possible codes include *L* for an item you learned in your teacher-education program, *SCH-G* for an item that reminds you of a pleasant experience you had

I feel good about myself when my students—

I feel bad about myself when my students—

I feel good about myself when other teachers—

I feel bad about myself when other teachers—

I feel discouraged about teaching when—

I feel encouraged about teaching when—

I feel I have been successful when—

I feel I have wasted students' time when—

I feel the students trust me when—

I feel the students are learning when—

I feel I am learning when—

I feel the students are not learning when—

I feel in a rut when—

I am glad to be a teacher when—

I lose my temper when—

I know it's time to put my foot down when—

I feel used when—

I like having classroom visitors when—

I am threatened when—

I am most patient in school when—

I am least patient in school when—

I am most at ease in school when—

I am least at ease in school when—

Students make me nervous when—

I react to other teachers—

I react to authority—

When I am in authority—

When people agree with me—

When people disagree with me—

Two things I can improve on as a teacher—

Three things I do exceptionally well as a teacher—

My students would describe me as—

My students' description of me makes me feel—

The student I like best—

The student I like least—

I listen—

I learn from my students—

when you were in the same grade as the one you are now teaching, or *SCH-B* for an unpleasant experience.

Repeat this activity at least four or five times over a period of a month or two. Do not read your past responses before you repeat this activity, since that might influence your completions. When you have done this activity a number of times and feel you have enough data, gather your worksheets and cut each sentence stem into a strip. Sort the strips according to the code in Worksheet 3. If you have modified the codes, change the worksheet accordingly. Next, examine each category on your worksheet by noting the sentences that have been grouped together. Then answer the following questions:

Questions

1. What similarities do you notice in each category?
2. What differences do you notice between categories?
3. Are there any recurring items that dominate each category?
4. Which category has the most responses? Which the least? What significance does the distribution of items over the worksheet have for you?
5. What areas of your professional life give you your greatest satisfactions as indicated by the worksheet? How can you expand these areas?
6. What areas of your professional life appear to be in need of modification? What steps can you begin to take?

Follow-up

Once you have identified the areas in your teaching life that you wish to change, the rest is up to you. You must be willing to make the investment in time and energy and to take responsibility for whatever changes you consider important. This is a very difficult task for all of us, however; New Year's resolutions are famous for being unfulfilled. One method of helping yourself change your behavior is to think of specific, direct steps that will accomplish your goal. You can then readily check to see how well you are succeeding. If you wish to be more self-disclosing, for example, you might resolve to talk about yourself at least twice each hour of the day. To further check your progress, repeat this activity after a month or so and notice what significant differences, if any, have occurred.

Worksheet 3

Place all P's here	Place all C's here	Place all UN's here	Place all ME's here	Place all NO's here	Place all D's here

Student Use

This is an easy activity to modify for use with students. Just change the sentence stems so that they are concerned with aspects of the students' lives. For example, "I feel bad when . . ." can be left as is, but you might change "My students might describe me as . . ." to "My friends might describe me as . . ." The rest of the activity remains the same, with modifications for different age groups. Older students can write and younger ones can finish the sentences orally in groups, with discussion following in either case.

SCHOOLBAG

What do you carry home from school each evening? Just as your wallet contains a great deal of information about you, so does the material you carry home and the container you carry it in. Empty the contents of your schoolbag (brief case, purse, knapsack, whatever you use) onto a table some evening and examine the contents and the bag itself.

1. What percentage of the work you carry home do you usually do?
2. What items in your schoolbag surprised you (that is, you weren't aware that they were there)?
3. Imagine that you found the bag and its contents and you do not know the owner. What do the bag and its contents tell you about the owner?

PERCEPTION GLASSES

Every perception is colored by the emotions, feelings, and thoughts of the moment; every situation can be viewed from various perspectives. For example, imagine that it is late afternoon on a rainy, cold day. Your day has been miserable, literally everything has gone wrong, and you feel about as depressed and cynical as you ever have. Then the phone rings, you answer, and you hear "Western Union calling. I have a telegram for (*you*)." How do you feel? What are your expectations?

Now imagine the situation reversed. It is a beautiful day, you are on top of the world, and you feel that absolutely everything and everybody is on your side. Again the phone rings, and again you hear, "Western Union calling. I have a telegram for (you)." How do you feel this time? What are your expectations?

Teachers view the classroom differently too, depending upon their current thoughts and feelings. Students' views are colored by their immediate concerns, and so too are supervisors affected by their personal and sometimes momentary perceptions. The following activity should heighten your awareness of the possible effects of your emotions, feelings, and thoughts of the moment upon your perceptions.

Objectives

1. To be aware of how emotions, feelings, and thoughts affect your perceptions.
2. To learn to view a situation from varying perspectives.

Directions

Arrange to observe a class taught by someone else. As you observe this class, try wearing a pair of imaginary glasses colored to reflect one dominant feeling, glasses that will force you to view the class from a single, narrow perspective, one that a student might have. You may use one of the following feelings or you may invent one of your own:

bored
enthusiastic
angry with teacher
angry with friend
scared
jealous
worried about the next period's exam

Wearing the imaginary glasses, observe the class for at least thirty minutes and record what you see. Note especially the dominant impressions you receive concerning the attitudes of those in the class.

Questions

1. How did the "glasses" you were wearing make you feel?
2. What observations did you make concerning the attitude of the teacher?
3. What were your dominant reactions to the students in the class?
4. Would you like to spend much time wearing those glasses?
5. What kind of "glasses" do you usually wear? What effect do they have on your perceptions? What effect do they have on those around you?

Follow-up

Observe the same class on another day, this time wearing a very different pair of glasses. How do your responses on this second day compare with those of your first observation?

What implications for your teaching can you draw as a result of your awareness of the effect your dominant feelings and attitudes have on your perceptions? For example, what does it mean in terms of your objectives for the day if a student is concerned with a family problem?

Variations for Use with Students

Students of all ages can learn the effect of their emotions and unique experiences on their perceptions. You might bring into school a number of pairs of sunglasses, each with different-colored lenses if possible. Explain that the person who wears a certain pair will also wear a very special way of looking at things. For example, we have all heard of the rose-colored glasses through which everything looks good and the world is on our side. Ask a volunteer to wear the rose-colored glasses, and ask him a series of questions while he is doing so. (How are you feeling today? What do you think the rest of the day will be like? How do most people feel about you?) His answers should reflect the mood he is wearing. When all the students understand the purpose of the glasses, have them select emotions that the glasses can represent (sad, suspicious, giddy, silly). Over a period of time, each student might be given the opportunity to wear a pair of glasses of his choice and to be questioned while wearing them. Your students may even want to make this into a game, with some students having to guess the tone imposed by the glasses. Obviously the wearer should be trying to help the guessers rather than fool them. Teams like those used in charades might be devised and a running score kept.

You can use the perception-glasses technique in content-oriented situations as well, particularly when you want students to understand that an event can be viewed from various perspectives. For example, a class studying a complex historical event might best understand the possibility of differing viewpoints by having various students, each wearing a different pair of "glasses," tell the class what he sees and how he feels about the situation. After reading about the facts of the Boston Tea Party, a student wearing "Indian" glasses might describe the event from his point of view, one wearing "Redcoat" glasses might do the same, and a third with "American-farmer" glasses could tell his side of the story. Literature, too, can be studied from the various perspectives of the characters in a novel, story, or play. Your imagination and that of your students is the only limitation on your use of this technique.

PERCEPTION COLLAGE

In many of the activities in this book you are asked to examine your perceptions of your teaching as a basis for self-analysis. While this skill is important, checking our perceptions with those of a learning partner who is familiar with our teaching is also helpful. The comparison between the two sets of perceptions can be powerful and fruitful feedback, providing that you are accepting, open, and nondefensive. A careful consideration of the similarities and differences in the two sets of perceptions can give you a more accurate picture of your teaching self.

Objectives

1. To compare your perceptions of your teaching self with those of an observer.
2. To consider the implications of any similarities and differences in the two sets of perceptions.

Directions

Ask a learning partner to watch a class when you are teaching a typical lesson. (At a later time you may wish to use this activity with an atypical lesson.) After the lesson both you and your partner fill in a separate worksheet about how you appeared in the lesson. (Prior to the lesson you might wish to add more descriptors to the worksheet to cover any aspects of your teaching that have not been included.) Do not collaborate or share your worksheets until you are both finished. Then compare the two worksheets and discuss the results.

Questions

1. About what aspects of your teaching do you agree? What does this tell you about your teaching? What agreements make you feel good? What agreements make you uncomfortable?
2. On what do you disagree? How do you account for these differences?
3. What factual data did each of you use for your decisions?
4. Which differences make you feel comfortable? uncomfortable?
5. What did you learn about your teaching from the discussion with your observer? What did you learn about your perceptions of your teaching?

Student Use

Devise for your students a worksheet that is concerned with an area of their life. For example, a worksheet might be concerned with relationships and might include such descriptors as *cooperative, friendly, stand-offish, selfish, generous, goes out of his way, a loner, popular, helpful,* and *curt.* Descriptors for a worksheet concerned with the role of a student might include *creative, hard-working, diligent, nonparticipating, quiet, turned off, enthusiastic, a leader,* and *aggressive.*

The students can choose partners with whom they are comfortable, and each partner then fills in a worksheet about his partner and one about

Worksheet

Circle all words that are appropriate descriptors for you. Add any descriptors you wish that are not included.

Creative

Exciting

Flexible

Impatient

Loving

Helpful

Flustered

Prepared

Positive

Demanding

Stationary

Fair

Open

Friendly

Closed

Student-centered

Well-dressed

Your Name

Stuffy

Spontaneous

Silly

Rigid

Bland

Fluid

Quiet

Teacher-centered   Lecturer

Caring

Powerful

Has favorites

Narrow-minded

Structured

Sarcastic   Knowledgable

Factual

himself. Once both worksheets are complete, each student can compare his worksheet about himself with that of his partner. Nondefensive discussion can follow. It is a good idea to remind the students that their partners' perceptions are not facts and need not be taken as truths. A different partner would have produced a different set of perceptions.

OBSERVATION: STUDENT POINT OF VIEW

Like many activities in this book, "Observation: Student Point of View" is based on the notion that we can learn a great deal about our profession through the eyes of our students. One reason for this seemingly obvious but often ignored phenomenon is that every decision we make regarding the classroom is based upon certain beliefs, including our beliefs about the students' mind-sets. We assume that we intuitively know how students will think, react, and feel about what we do in the classroom. These beliefs, if we don't verify them, become fantasies that may or may not be true. A single fantasy might not create too serious a distortion, but each fantasy can add to the distance between student and teacher, and the effects can accumulate into a serious reality gap. We must constantly recognize this phenomenon and work to verify our fantasies against the reality they could so easily supplant.

In the diagram below, Fig. 3.1 describes a situation in which the student's reality (S) and the teacher's idea of the student's reality (T) are separate. The teacher has not checked out his fantasy of the student's reality, and the student has not shared his reality with the teacher. There is no reality-base between them. In Fig. 3.2 a small portion of the student's reality is shared with the teacher, either because the student shared it or because the teacher validated part of his fantasy with the student. As the student shares more of his reality and as the teacher validates

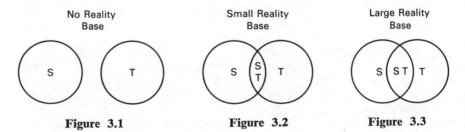

No Reality	Small Reality	Large Reality
Base	Base	Base

Figure 3.1   **Figure 3.2**   **Figure 3.3**

S = Student's view of what T = Teacher's view of what
is happening to him.   is happening to the students.

more of his fantasy, a large reality base is established, as depicted in Fig. 3.3, and the teacher better understands the student's reality.

In order to make realistic and effective decisions, a teacher must have large reality areas and small fantasy areas (as shown in the above diagram). While it is not possible to achieve a total reality base, the teacher can be in a constant state of closing the gap, as diagrammed below:

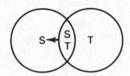

One way to close the gap is to constantly check your assumptions with your students to see if they are accurate. Many activities in this book provide structured mechanisms to check out assumptions. In addition, you may ask students direct questions for feedback on the accuracy of your assumptions. Other activities provide data on your assumptions by having you draw on your experiences as a student.

"Observation: Student Point of View" is a classroom observation exercise that takes place in the here and now. You are asked to experience a class just as a student would so that you can have a chance to substantiate some of your fantasies.

Objectives

1. To sit in an actual classroom and observe from the point of view of a student.
2. To respond to a set of scales about the class from the student point of view.
3. To be able to use the student point of view as a feedback device in looking at your lessons.

Directions

Sit in a class in your school (visit a class in a nearby school if you are not teaching). As you sit there, imagine yourself as a student in that class. Sit in a student's desk, feel the desktop under your hand and the floor under your feet. Try to get in touch with how it must feel to be a student in this class. Imagine that all teacher directions are meant for you (do not actually respond, but imagine how you might respond). Then, as you sit there, look down the sets of descriptors on the accompanying

Worksheet   **Student Point of View**

Indicate your reactions concerning the atmosphere of the class on each scale.

CONCENTRATION _____ DISTRACTION

BUSY _____ DELAYING

EXCITEMENT _____ BOREDOM

DOING _____ POSTPONING

TALKATIVE _____ UNEXPRESSIVE

FREEDOM _____ RESTRICTION

CONTINUITY _____ INTERRUPTIONS

FRESHNESS _____ REPETITION

CONSENT _____ DENIAL

For your own use, make lists of descriptors specifically designed to provide feed-back about something you are especially concerned with in your classes.

worksheet. After the class, mark on each scale your immediate reaction to each set of descriptors as you think a student in that class might respond. On the bottom of the worksheet list some of the actual events that occurred in the class that are responsible for the way you fill in the scales.

Follow-up Activity

After teaching a class or lesson of your own, fill in the same set of scales in the method described above. Imagine that you are a student in your class. You might even think of certain students who participated in the lesson and fill out the scales as you imagine they would. Use quiet and active students, bored and excited students, and other student types in your room. To validate your perceptions, ask students to fill out the scales and compare their responses with yours.

Another alternative is to ask your observer to sit in the class and mark the scales from the student point of view. Discuss your observer's perceptions at the conclusion of the lesson. This activity is most valuable when repeated from time to time. Keep a record of your evaluations and how they measured up to another's perception, either student or observer or both. Try to work toward making accurate perceptions about your students. Always validate your perceptions by asking students to reveal their reality.

Follow-up Questions

1. In comparing your perceptions with those of the students or an observer, did you find yourself to be highly accurate, highly inaccurate, or somewhere in between? What do these results mean to you?
2. Are you pleased or displeased with the implications about your teaching that are raised by this activity? Why?
3. What, specifically, might you do differently as a result of this activity? How will you begin to do it?
4. What can you do to become an accurate observer with realistic perceptions of the student point of view?

SCHOOL PARADOXES

Like every institution, schools are filled with paradoxes and ironies. For example, we know a government teacher who extols the virtues of democracy but demands strict obedience from his students, who are never asked for input and certainly never experience the democratic process in his class. We also have known students who vocally support student-rights movements demanding freedom and independence but who act dependently on both adults and peers. Just recently we visited a school that is based on an open-classroom philosophy. The students design their own curricula and work independently, but they wear uniforms. Student creativity is a major topic of conversation there, but all the bulletin boards are products of teacher efforts. We also know a first-grade teacher whose stated major goal is developing responsibility, but she lines her children up to go to the bathroom at the same time every day.

Objectives

1. To be aware of paradoxes and ironies in your school.
2. To determine which paradoxes and ironies in your school you may be able to control.

Directions

Keep a record on the accompanying worksheet of all the paradoxes you find in your school. You can do this independently, keeping notes over a period of a couple of days in which you consciously seek out the paradoxes. You could also involve your students or a group of colleagues in brainstorming the list (see pp. 14–15).

In the spaces to the right on the worksheet, code the paradoxes according to the following scheme:

1. Use a *T* to indicate those for which teachers are responsible, an *A* for those for which the administration is responsible, and an *S* for those for which students are responsible.
2. In the second column rank the practices according to how much each one bothers or concerns you. Put a *1* next to the one that concerns you most, and so on.

Questions

1. Who—administrators, teachers, or students—are responsible for most of the paradoxes in your school? Over which of these paradoxes do you have some control?
2. Do you find any of the paradoxes you listed to be healthy? Are any of them fun? Are there any that you want to preserve?

Paradoxes	T-A-S	Ranking

3. Do the three paradoxes that you ranked as being of the most concern to you have anything in common with one another? If so, what?

4. What can and will you do to eliminate one of the paradoxes that bothers you?

CLASSROOM ARRANGEMENT

The arrangement of any room, especially a classroom, has a significant impact on the interaction that occurs in that room. Your teaching style and beliefs about learning are reflected in the arrangement that you select and use. No one arrangement is best in all situations. An arrangement that excludes the teacher from the students will have a different effect on student-teacher interaction than an arrangement that places the teacher in more intimate contact with the students. Likewise, a student's placement in relation to other students has a significant effect on the interaction between students. Often we have not carefully examined the effects of the arrangements we use or attempted to relate them to our goals. We simply adopted those we knew as students or have seen used by colleagues.

The following activity is adapted from research [1] for the purpose of encouraging you to consider different classroom arrangements and their possible effects on the human interaction that occurs. The most important aspect of this activity is not to eliminate any classroom arrangement, but to expand the number of arrangements that are available for your choice. You must be careful not to prejudge and close your mind to the many possibilities that exist for you. Each arrangement can serve you when used with an understanding of the consequences.

Objectives

1. To consider different classroom arrangements as alternatives for use in your room.

2. To expand the possible choices of classroom arrangement.

3. To determine which classroom arrangements can best serve your teaching purposes.

[1] Fred C. Feitler, "Teacher's Desk." Reprinted from "Tie Line" by Kenneth Goodall in *Psychology Today*, Vol. 5, No. 4, September 1971, p. 12. Copyright © Communications/Research/Machines, Inc.

Directions

Study the different types of classroom arrangements described on the worksheets. Note that O represents the students' location and X the teacher's location. During the study portion of this activity defer judgment on any arrangement. Remember that at any time during your teaching you may wish to use different arrangements. By keeping each of the alternatives open and understanding how teaching effectiveness is related to each arrangement, you will be better able to move smoothly from one alternative to another. Try to imagine what each arrangement looks like in an actual classroom. Imagine what kinds of activities are facilitated by each arrangement, and what kinds of activities are hindered. On the following worksheets list under each arrangement the kinds of activities that are best-suited to the arrangement and those that are ill-suited. The next time you draw up your lesson plans or do activity planning, think of how the arrangement can play a facilitating role in the lesson. Decide which arrangement serves you best and use it in the classroom.

Questions

1. Which of the seven arrangements have you experienced as a student?
2. In which of these arrangements are you most comfortable as a student? Why? As a teacher? Why?
3. In which are you least comfortable as a student? Why? As a teacher? Why?
4. Which arrangements have you observed in classrooms you have visited? What is your overall impression of the environment created by each as you have experienced or seen it?
5. Which arrangement is primarily used in the classroom you are now working in? What effect does this arrangement have on the atmosphere or tone of the classroom?
6. What other arrangements can you think of as alternatives to the seven on the worksheets? Include these in your deliberations in this activity.

Follow-up

Now that you have considered different classroom arrangements, it's time to experiment with them. Try each arrangement as both teacher

Worksheet 1

Setting One

Facilitates   Hinders

Comments:

○ = Student location   **X** = Teacher location

Worksheet 2

Setting Two

Facilitates   Hinders

Comments:

◯ = Student location   **X** = Teacher location

Worksheet 3

Setting Three

X

○○○○○○
○○○○○○
○○○○○○
○○○○○○

Facilitates   Hinders

Comments:

O = Student location   **X** = Teacher location

Worksheet 4

Setting Four

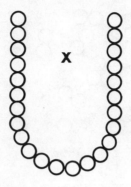

Facilitates   Hinders

Comments:

◯ = Student location   **X** = Teacher location

Worksheet 5

Setting Five
(no teacher)

Facilitates   Hinders

Comments:

○ = Student location   **X** = Teacher location

Worksheet 6

Setting Six

○ ○ ○ ○ ○ ○
○ ○ ○ ○ ○ ○
○ ○ ○ ○ **X** ○
○ ○ ○ ○ ○ ○

Facilitates   Hinders

Comments:

○ = Student location   **X** = Teacher location

Worksheet 7

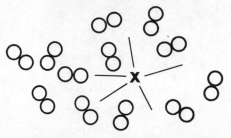

Setting Seven
(teacher moves freely)

Facilitates   Hinders

Comments:

O = Student location   **X** = Teacher location

(with your class on varying days) and as student (possibly through the use of role-playing). Were your perceptions and conclusions about each arrangement accurate? Change any information on the worksheets that is disproved through actual practice. You can get additional feedback from your students by giving each of them a worksheet and asking them to state which are most and least comfortable for them. Compare their worksheets with yours. In your journal keep a record of each arrangement that you use in your teaching (or those you observe) and note how the arrangement may have affected the process of the lesson.

LOG CONVERSATION: LESSON PLANS

Rick: Every time I visit a new school, I become aware of how important specific rituals are to the life of that school.

Barbara: Can you give me an example?

Rick: Well, Silberman gives a good one in *Crisis in the Classroom* about lesson plans.

> The tyranny of the lesson plan in turn encourages an obsession with routine for the sake of routine. School is filled with countless examples of teachers and administrators confusing means with ends, thereby making it impossible to reach the end for which the means were devised.[2]

I bet that a lesson plan can be a real hindrance when it becomes ritualistic. Do you readers agree?

You:

Barbara: But lesson plans can help me at times. Can they help you?

You:

---

[2] Charles Silberman, *Crisis in the Classroom* (New York: Random House, 1970), p. 125.

Rick: What do you think makes a lesson plan a hindrance and what makes it helpful?

You:

RITUALS

In every classroom and every school particular practices, such as the morning announcements or the greeting a teacher gives her class, have a tendency to become ritualistic. They become expected practice, not because they serve a useful and consciously chosen purpose, but because they have become a part of the school. Although the practice originally may have developed to meet a need, it becomes a ritual when it loses its contact with the base from which it developed and is practiced simply because it always has been. For example, many teachers begin each new year by seating students according to a seating chart developed in order to facilitate the teacher's learning the students' names. The arrangement has a useful purpose. But if the teacher continues to insist that students sit according to the chart long after he has learned the names, and if he has no other reason for using that arrangement, then the seating arrangement has become ritualistic. It exists for no other reason than to perpetuate itself and therefore is an irrational aspect of that classroom in the eyes of the students.

Not all rituals, of course, have the negative influence of a rigid and meaningless seating chart. Some, like special meals on special days or the wearing of unusual clothes for celebrations of one sort of another, may be fun and can serve to build a community spirit among the participants. It is important, however, to become aware of the rituals in your classroom and school so that you can control them, rather than allowing them to control you.

Objectives

1. To be aware of ritualistic tendencies in your school and classroom.
2. To control the ritualistic aspects of your classroom.

Directions

To become aware of the rituals in your school, invent a new holiday. Select one from the list below or make up a new one. Then, with your students or a group of colleagues, brainstorm (see "Brainstorming," pp. 14–15) a list of all the ways your school and classrooms would probably celebrate that day.

Possible new holidays: Broccoli Day, Sunshine Day, Spaghetti Day, Barefoot Day, Influenza Day, Hair Day, Parking-Ticket Day, Transylvania Day, Curl Day, Cockatoo Day, Popsicle Day, Eat-With-Your-Fingers Day, Toe Day, Flashlight Day, Grasshopper Day, Plastic Day, Broken-Pencil Day, Tongue-in-Cheek Day.

From the list of ways the new holiday might be celebrated, select those you would enjoy and approve, and compile a new list. Then do the same for those you would not enjoy or approve. Compare your list with those of others who have also compiled such lists. (If you produced lists with your students, you might ask them how they can use this information to make their life in school more meaningful and enjoyable. They might decide to try to eliminate a longstanding but insignificant practice, or they might try to institute a new practice that they see as worthwhile or fun.)

Now take a look with your students at your classroom, and generate a list of rituals in your room. Include both academic practices (quiz on Friday and standard headings required on papers turned in) and non-academic practices (bulletin boards changed on the first of the month and separate lines for boys and girls when leaving the room). Write this list of classroom rituals on the accompanying worksheet. Then, in the spaces at the right, code each ritual according to the following scheme:

1. If the activity builds community spirit in the classroom, indicate this with a *CS* for Community Spirit. Otherwise leave blank.

2. If you were responsible for the activity, indicate this with *I*. If it was there before you, use *O* for other.

3. Use an *S* to indicate those that students support, an *R* for those which they resist.

4. Indicate how often the ritual occurs:
   H for hourly
   D for daily
   W for weekly
   M for monthly
   Y for yearly

Classroom Rituals	CS	I-O	S-R	H-D-W-M-Y	E-U	P	C	UNIQ	GU	Other

5. Use an *E* for those that are enjoyable, a *U* for those that are un-enjoyable.

6. Use a *P* to indicate those rituals that require preparation.

7. Use a *C* if the ritual allows for creativity.

8. Use *UNIQ* if the ritual is, in your school, unique to your room.

9. Use *GU* to indicate those classroom rituals you are willing to give up.

10. Use this column to categorize your classroom rituals by some other criteria.

Questions

1. How do the rituals in your classroom serve you?

2. What factors contribute to your willingness to give up those you checked in column nine on the worksheet? Is it important to you to give up any of these? If so, which?

3. Do any of the rituals noted on your worksheet limit your behavior in any way?

4. How can you insure that meaningful activities do not lose their context and become ritualistic?

5. How do your students respond to rituals in your classroom? Ask them for feedback about which they like, dislike, would like to eliminate. Ask them also to suggest new practices, with meaning and purpose, to substitute for ones that are no longer useful.

STUDENT PAPERS

Most teachers spend many hours each week responding in writing to the written work of students. We check over papers done in class, look at and respond to students' homework, and write lengthy comments on the original work created both in and out of class. We are continuing a practice that all of us became familiar with when we were students; the red-pencil syndrome has been deeply and thoroughly established in American schools. Also well-established is the practice of most students of paying little or no attention to the responses so laboriously made by us, the teachers. We have often heard the teacher comment "Why should I spend so much time correcting papers? They never use the corrections constructively anyway! In fact, if I don't require them to go over the corrections in class, most of them wouldn't even look at them."

love is...

... saying "I feel differently" instead of "you're wrong."

Students don't look at the corrections, but why should they? We don't enjoy having our weak points and mistakes paraded before us, and neither do students. Unfortunately, however, most of the comments that teachers put on student papers serve to destroy rather than enhance the student's self-concept. Our young people as they grow up will (and should) make every effort to build positive images of themselves. No wonder they try to ignore or downgrade anything that tells them they are less than worthy. The human organism won't survive healthily in a hostile environment, and many of our teacher-made comments and corrections, however subtly, constitute a hostile environment.

The following activity offers you an opportunity to evaluate the comments you have made on student papers to determine their possible destructive and constructive impacts on students.

Objectives

1. To differentiate constructive and destructive comments.
2. To use constructive comments effectively.

Directions

Most of the comments that teachers write on student work can be classified into one of ten categories. Five are generally destructive in that they point out errors, apparently for no other reason than to show the student his inadequacies. The other five are constructive in that they support the student's efforts and offer specific assistance. The destructive comments tear students apart; the constructive ones help them build their skills and self-confidence.

DESTRUCTIVE COMMENTS

1. *Simple corrections.* Mistakes are indicated by a mark, usually a X or a √ in red. A glance is all that is needed for a student to measure his inadequacy.

2. *Vague references to needed improvement with no specifications of what is needed.* Often a question mark or a vague reference like *unclear, poor,* or *vague* is written in a margin. The student is given no assistance in understanding the reference or how to improve.

3. *Comments that indicate the teacher's disagreement but do not provide factual data.* The student is told that he is wrong but not why he is wrong, or he is told that his opinion is unacceptable. Comments like *No, Your thinking is fuzzy,* and *Experts disagree,* especially in matters of opinion, are examples.

4. *Sarcastic put-downs. Sure!, Oh really? Come on, now, You don't say!,* and similar statements serve only to threaten the student by telling him his ideas are unacceptable.

5. *Prescriptive corrections (usually in red) of spelling, punctuation, grammar, and other skills, when they are used as the focus of the comments.* Students, especially those who are unsure of their skills to begin with, are taught only that they are hopeless failures. (These do not include judicious and meaningful suggestions and help in these skill areas.)

CONSTRUCTIVE COMMENTS

1. *Personal reactions in which a dialogue between student and teacher is initiated.* Examples: *This idea excites me; Your account of your anger here brought back vivid memories of a similar situation in my life; I'm not sure I understand you here, let's talk about it.*

2. *Specific suggestions for improvement in which the emphasis is not on what is wrong, but on what can be done to improve.* Examples: *This argument will be stronger if you use specific examples; How did this event follow from the one preceding it? Show the relationship clearly.*

3. *Questions designed to extend the student's thinking, especially on the meaning of events and information to him.* Examples: *Is this bit of knowledge important to you? How? How has this opinion affected your life? How difficult is it for you to uphold this opinion? How has this discovery been important to you?*

4. *Corrections of grammar, spelling, punctuation, and other skills that are used sparingly for the purpose of clarifying thought.* No more than two such corrections on any one paper can probably be assimilated. Unlike the prescriptive corrections indicated previously, which are used simply to show students their mistakes, the focus here is on improving the meaning through better writing, not on pointing out errors.

5. *Specific supportive comments that indicate progress and recognize achievement.* Examples: *You've become much clearer in organizing your presentation; This is an excellent use of metaphor!* General supportive comments like *good* and *well-done,* though not destructive, are not so constructive as more specific comments that provide definite and meaningful feedback.

Consider this actual composition written by an eighth-grade student on the theme "What Is My Ideal School?" The composition is first corrected with primarily destructive comments, and then is corrected again using constructive comments. Notice the differences in the tone and helpfulness in the two sets of comments.

With Destructive Comments:

My school would be in Aspen Colorado.
Students would be in Junior High ages
12-14 grades 7-9. This would not be a
word? religious nor strictly white or black.
You must be able to speak English. The
amount of students would not be over 800. *awk.*
The system would be Modular Scheduling.
frag. Mods being 15 minutes apiece. Students
would choose their own schedule 3 months   *awk.*
at the changing of marking periods. The
grades will not be A, B, or C, They'll be   *poor sentence —*
S—which stands for Satisfactory. NI—   *rewrite*
which stands for needs improvement, when
getting needs to improve, depending on
the subject you you got an NI on you'd have

to come after school. 3 days a week, during
the next marking period.

frag.

When making your schedule you would
have a list of classes to schedule. In
making a 7 and ½ hour day, 5 days a week,
9 months in a year.

these are not sentences — fix

Ski instruction would be 2 hours,
leisure skiing 1 hour. 3 mods of study hall
for homework. 2 mods of math. 1 hour and
15 minutes of specified options. The
specified options would include Art,
Home Ec, Industrial Arts, Foreign
language, gym, swimming, Instrumental
lessons, chorus. Students then have an
option of social classes like social
studies to science classes. English
options would also be avaible.

frag.

— frag.

no caps

— awk.

why only these

— spelling

Teachers would not be over 42 in age.
They must all ski.

Good teachers don't have to ski.

With Constructive Comments:

My school would be in Aspen Colorado.
Students would be in Junior High ages
12-14 grades 7-9. This would not be a
religious nor strictly white or black.
You must be able to speak English. The
amount of students would not be over 800.

I'm impressed with your admission policy. Do you know of any schools that have different ones?

The system would be Modular Scheduling, WITH
Mods being 15 minutes apiece.
Students would choose their own schedule
3 months at the changing of marking
periods. The grades will not be A, B, or
C, They'll be S-which stands for
Satisfactory, or NI-which stands for
needs improvement, when getting needs to
improve, depending on the subject you
you got an NI on you'd have to come after
school. 3 days a week, during the next
marking period.

These are fragments. Try joining together the phrases by commas to make one sentence. Notice how I did it.

why is your grading system better than ours? How would it help you?

When making your schedule you would
have a list of classes to schedule. In
making a 7 and ½ hour day, 5 days a week,

9 months in a year.

Ski instruction would be 2 hours, leisure skiing 1 hour. 3 mods of study hall for homework. 2 mods of math. 1 hour and 15 minutes of specified options. The specified options would include Art, Home Ec, Industrial Arts, Foreign language, gym, swimming, Instrumental lessons, chorus. Students then have an option of social classes like social studies to science classes. English options would also be avaible.

Teachers would not be over 42 in age. They must all ski.

[Handwritten margin note, left: If you were a student in your school, could you help teach skiing?]

[Handwritten margin notes, right: Can you find and correct the sentence fragments? I would like to go to your school. Can you imagine what it's like to be 44, who do you know that's 44. Are they retired?]

Using the ten categories, analyze the comments you wrote on at least ten student papers. You can use your most recent batch of papers or you can ask students to return old papers and choose some at random. Copy each comment you made onto the accompanying worksheet. Then classify each one as either destructive or constructive. You can also categorize them by type, using the numbers of the ten types in the list, if you wish.

Questions

1. Add up the number of destructive comments and the number of constructive comments. What do these numbers say to you about the comments you put on these papers?
2. Which kind of comments, destructive or constructive, is easier for you to make? What does that mean to you?
3. Pick out three comments that you classified as destructive. What do you imagine the students' reactions to these might have been? Rewrite each as a constructive comment.
4. What implications does this activity have for you?

Follow-up

On the next set of papers that you collect, make only constructive comments. When you return the papers to your students, you might choose to tell them that you have attempted to use only constructive responses. Point out the kind of comments you have made and explain the rationale for doing so. Observe student reactions to the comments and keep a record of their responses.

Worksheet

COMMENT

Student Papers

TYPE

Student Use

"Put-downs" are a common mode of interaction among students. Although they often react to such comments with laughter, the laughter itself is a thin covering for the hurt that is felt. Put-downs heard frequently in schools include unkind nicknames, like "Fatso" or "Bucky," and comments like "The teacher's pet always gets A's," "If I had your looks I'd never use a mirror," and "Who are *you* going to the party with?" The best list of put-downs frequently heard in your school will be generated by your students. After discussing with them the use and effect of put-downs, have them brainstorm a list of put-downs they have heard, used, or can imagine. Post the list in a conspicuous place in the room. Encourage students to avoid using the put-downs on the list.

If you and your students wish, you might even outlaw the use of put-downs in your room. If you do so, be careful that those who err and use a put-down are treated gently and acceptantly and are not put-down in turn; instead, use support and encouragement to help them find a better way to express themselves. Sharing your attempts to eliminate put-downs from your conversations and written responses will help students in their attempts to do the same.

IDENTIFYING FEELINGS

What goes on in a classroom is affected by many factors: physical influences like the size, shape, and decor of the room; type and flexibility of furniture; materials available; quality of heat and light; managerial influences, including established procedures and administrative style; influences arising from the unique characteristics of the students; influences arising from the unique characteristics of the teacher.

We must be able to determine for ourselves how these and other forces are affecting our classrooms. We must then determine which of them we can control, wholly or in part, and which we cannot. We can then, and only then, manipulate the classroom environment so that it meets student needs as much as possible. Depending upon your situation, you may have much, little, or no influence on many factors. This only you can determine. For example, if you are in a traditional egg-crate type of classroom, you have little or no control over the size and shape of your room (unless you also have some movable partitions). If you are in a new open-space building, you probably have considerable say about the size and shape of learning environments for your students. If you are a first-year teacher in a large system, you will probably spend a full year just learning the various administrative procedures and will most likely have little or no influence on them during this year, but if you are a veteran teacher on a small staff, you probably have a considerable influence. If you are also a good friend of the principal or superintendent, of course, you may increase your degree of influence over administrative procedure commensurately.

One area that we alone control, however, is the influence on our classroom of our internal states—our attitudes, concerns, and feelings of the moment. Though we may argue that external events contribute to our feelings, we cannot escape full responsibility for the effect of our feelings on our students and on our effectiveness as teachers. If you feel open, spontaneous, and responsive while teaching, the chances that your students will respond in a similar manner are significantly increased. If you feel closed, rigid, and uncaring, you can be sure your students will perceive your feelings and respond accordingly. Thus a cycle is set up: if you are bored, surely your students will sense your boredom and respond with boredom; you sense their boredom, which then reinforces yours. The outcome, naturally, is boredom for everyone, and unless you sense it and change the climate, the class will be deadly. Conversely, when you are truly excited (not faking it), your excitement is likely to infect at least some students, who will also become excited. Your excitement is rewarded and reinforced, and you and your students are off!

Because our feelings have such a great impact on what happens in our classrooms, it is often helpful for us to identify what our feelings are in particular situations and to relate them to what is happening. The following activity, which you can do alone or with the help of an observer, is offered to help you identify your feelings.

Objectives

1. To identify how you felt while teaching a particular lesson.
2. To collect data on which to base an analysis of how your feelings affected the lesson.
3. To compare the way you felt with the way you appeared to an observer.

Directions

On the following pages are worksheets containing sets of continua. Each continuum represents a range of feelings between two extremes. Immediately following a lesson or class, simply run down one of the

worksheets with a pencil, marking how you *felt* in that class on each of
the scales. Your placement of a mark on each scale should be determined
by your immediate reaction to that set of adjectives. Don't puzzle over
individual items. It is the immediate feeling about yourself in the situation you just experienced that is important.

If you wish to work with your observer, select one of the scales prior
to teaching a lesson. During the lesson the observer should mark on each
continuum how he judges your behavior. After the lesson you mark an
identical scale as directed above. Then compare the two sets of scales and
discuss the implications of any similarities and differences you find.

Questions

1. Are you pleased with the way you felt during the lesson? Why or
   why not?
2. What factors, internal or external, contributed to your feelings and
   behavior?
3. What effect did your feelings have on your lesson, your students, or
   your classroom as a whole?
4. What, if anything, would you like to change? How will you begin
   to do it?

Discuss with the observer:

1. How do your continua compare? Note especially any continuum on
   which your analyses differ. Attempt to discover what factors were
   operating in each of your judgments.
2. Which of the continua are most significant for you? Why?
3. How can the two of you work together to implement your answer
   to number four above?

Follow-up

A. If by doing this exercise you have identified an area you want to
work on, or if you just want to monitor your feelings over a period of
time, continue using the same set of scales at weekly or twice-weekly
intervals over no less than six weeks. Date each set and put down a
notation that will remind you of the circumstances of that particular
lesson—for example, "mapping the route of Columbus, 6/5, 1 P.M."
When you have collected between six and twelve scales, lay them side by
side in chronological order and compare them.

Identifying Feelings

OPEN _____ CLOSED

HOPEFUL _____ HOPELESS

CAREFUL _____ SLOPPY

SEXY_____ SEXLESS

DEMANDING _____ ACCEPTING

LISTLESS _____ ACTIVE

HERE AND NOW _____ THERE AND THEN

HOSTILE _____ CARING

HUMAN _____ MECHANISTIC

EXPERIMENTAL _____ RITUALISTIC

COLD _____ WARM

FEARFUL _____ CONFIDENT

CONSISTENT _____ INCONSISTENT

GUILTY _____ PROUD

EMPATHETIC _____ SELF-ABSORBED

CLOSE _____ DISTANT

FULL _____ EMPTY

I _____ WE

AWARE _____ UNAWARE

PLANNED _____ SPONTANEOUS

TEACHER ROLE _____ MYSELF

SERIOUS _____ FLIPPANT

AIMLESS _____ PURPOSEFUL

LIKED _____ DISLIKED

BORED _____ ENTHUSIASTIC

TRADITIONAL _____ INNOVATIVE

PERSONAL _____ AUTHORITARIAN

CONGRUENT _____ INCONGRUENT

AWARE _____ UNAWARE

HAPPY _____ SAD

1. What feelings remained markedly consistent over the duration? What does this consistency mean to you?
2. What feelings fluctuated? What does this fluctuation mean?
3. What changes have occurred? Are they lasting changes?
4. What implications does the record before you have for your teaching?

B. You might also use feeling-identification continua to compare two very different situations in which you find yourself. Perhaps you work with two groups of students and each group responds differently to you. In this case it might be instructive to have your observer complete a set of scales detailing the way he sees you in each of those classes. You can then compare the scales and draw implications for your teaching in those two situations.

Student Use

Students of all ages can be made aware of how their feelings affect their environments, and you can help them. With young children you might simply be on the alert for opportunities to ask them how they feel and how their feelings affect what's going on around them. Older students who are interested in self-awareness can use scales like those included here to identify their feelings and the effects of their feelings in specific situations—when giving a speech, working in a small group, working out a problem with friends, negotiating an issue with parents, when asked to assume a leadership role, or at any other time the student chooses. The analysis following the activity should focus on identifying the factors that contributed to the ratings, judging the possible effects of those feelings, identifying the ratings the student would like to change, and discussing how the changes might be brought about.

LOG CONVERSATION: "TRALFAMADORE"

Rick: I just reread one of my favorite novels, *The Sirens of Titan,* by Kurt Vonnegut. I noticed again how much that novel speaks to me as an educator. I especially like the following passage:

Once upon a time on Tralfamadore there were creatures who weren't anything like machines. They weren't dependable. They weren't efficient. They weren't predictable. They weren't durable. And these poor creatures were obsessed by the idea that everything that existed had to have a purpose, and that some purposes were higher than others.

These creatures spent most of their time trying to find out what their purpose was. And every time they found out what seemed to be a purpose of themselves, the purpose seemed so low that the creatures were filled with disgust and shame.

And, rather than serve such a low purpose, the creatures would make a machine to serve it. This left the creatures to serve higher purposes. But whenever they found a higher purpose, the purpose still wasn't high enough.

So the machines were made to serve higher purposes too.

And the machines did everything so expertly that they were finally given the job of finding out what the highest purpose of the creatures could be.

The machines reported in all honesty that the creatures couldn't really be said to have any purpose at all.

The creatures thereupon began slaying each other, because they hated purposeless things above all else.

And they discovered that they weren't even very good at slaying. So they turned that job over to the machines, too. And the machines finished up the job in less time than it takes to say, "Tralfamadore." [3]

Barbara: I see what you mean. I often get so wrapped up in identifying purposes and meeting goals that I miss the joy of the moment because I am unaware of the present. It says something to me about establishing purposes for my students too. I wonder what meaning you readers make of the passage?

You:

Rick: When I question purposes, I also have to question what it is to be an effective teacher. Can you readers relate your concept of effective teaching to what the passage says about purposes?

You:

---

[3] Kurt Vonnegut, Jr., *The Sirens of Titan.* Copyright © 1959 by Kurt Vonnegut, Jr. A Seymour Lawrence Book/Delacorte Press. Used by permission of the publisher. Pp. 274–75.

CLASSROOM EFFECTIVENESS

For each activity that is occurring in your classroom, you probably have some identifiable goals. It is likely that these goals, at least insofar as they concern the students, are quite clear in your mind, whether or not they are written into a lesson plan. For example, if you are working with a group of students on a mathematical concept, you most likely have identified an objective: *The student shall be able to correctly add a series of eight digits.* It is a relatively simple matter to evaluate the effectiveness of the activity by giving the students a series of eight digits and asking them to add them.

But how do you evaluate your behavior as teacher in the class? Do you have goals for yourself, and if so, have you articulated them and put them into operation in any way? You have as much responsibility, we think, for examining, evaluating, and changing your behavior as you do for examining, evaluating, and attempting to change the behavior of your students. But to do this effectively, you must identify some personal goals for yourself. You then must devise a way to measure your effectiveness in reaching those goals. The following activity should be of some assistance in these important tasks.

Objectives

1. To describe specific teaching behaviors that you consider positive qualities.
2. To gather feedback concerning those specific teaching behaviors you consider important.

Directions

Before teaching a lesson or a class, sit down with your observer and outline your goals for the lesson. Include not only your goals for the students, but your intentions concerning your behavior in the class as well. From the list of personal goals, select the one or two that are the most important for you. With the observer's assistance, describe how that behavior could be demonstrated. For example, if you decide that you want to be helpful, you might decide that a helpful teacher is one who—

displays concern for all students;
accepts all viewpoints;

encourages divergent opinions;

supports even the sketchiest of ideas;

respects every opinion;

uses positive responses.

Together with the observer, list as many concrete behaviors that demonstrate your behavioral goal as you can. Then list behaviors that characterize the opposite of the goal. For example, the opposite of *helpful* might be *hindering*, which happens when a teacher—

cuts students off;

favors "right" answers;

rejects divergent opinions;

ignores student requests;

"puts down" students.

After you and your observer have specified both positive and negative behaviors, the observer can record and classify on the accompanying worksheet all instances of such behavior that you display in a class. To continue our example, the observer might note down "cut Sally off in midsentence when Sally offered silly response" and classify it as "probably hindering."

After you have taught the lesson or the class and the observer has noted and classified behaviors, you and the observer can use this data to analyze your effectiveness in the area under consideration. You might then record your evaluation of your effectiveness by indicating on a continuum that expresses the whole range of possible behavior where you feel your behavior lay in that particular instance. For the example of helpfulness, the continuum would look like the following:

extremely	quite	moderately	moderately	quite	extremely
helpful	helpful	helpful	hindering	hindering	hindering

Be sure to indicate also the date on which the lesson was taught, and give yourself some reminder as to what the lesson was about and what made it unique.

The example used above is only a suggestion. Your own experience will tell you what area to scrutinize. You might decide to examine your behavior with regard to self-assurance, fairness, or sensitivity, for example. Here are two others to further illustrate how to set up a continuum.

Specific Behavior   Classification
_____

FLEXIBILITY

extremely	quite	moderately	moderately	quite	extremely
flexible	flexible	flexible	inflexible	inflexible	inflexible

SENSE OF HUMOR

always uses and	usually uses and	sometimes uses and	seldom uses or	never uses or
appreciates humor	appreciates humor	appreciates humor	appreciates humor	appreciates humor

Follow-up

If you have discovered an aspect of your teaching self with which you are less than completely satisfied (and who among us is perfect?), you have ahead of you the difficult and time-consuming task of changing yourself. You can help yourself by continually using your observer to collect data on your behavior, by analyzing that data openly and nondefensively, and by designing new behaviors and planning ways to incorporate them into your daily teaching. Analyze your behavior in a particular area like helpfulness repeatedly over a period of time and use the same continuum to evaluate your behavior each time. Dating each evaluation on the continuum will provide you with a progress chart. Remember that significant change is slow and arduous; give yourself time and allow yourself mistakes. Only with consistent effort and a spirit of acceptance will you make the progress you hope for, but the prize is worth the effort.

LOG CONVERSATION: GOOD LEARNERS

Barbara: Not until rather recently have I been concerned with what it means to me to be a learner. People have been pushing and pulling me most of my life, giving me answers and their prescriptions for living. I'm now in the process of defining learning. Postman and Weingartner have offered one description that speaks to me:

What do good learners believe? What do good learners do?
First, good learners have *confidence* in their ability to learn. This does

not mean that they are not sometimes frustrated and discouraged. They are, even as are poor learners. But they have a profound faith that they are capable of solving problems, and if they fail at one problem, they are not incapacitated in confronting another.

Good learners tend to *enjoy* solving problems. The process interests them, and they tend to resent people who want to "help" by giving them the answers.

Good learners seem to know what is relevant to their survival and what is not. They are apt to resent being told that something is "good for them to know," unless, of course, their crap detector advises them that it *is* good for them to know—in which case, they resent being told anyway.

Good learners, in other words, prefer to rely on their own judgment. They recognize, especially as they grow older, that an incredible number of people do not know what they are talking about most of the time. As a consequence, they are suspicious of "authorities," especially any authority who discourages others from relying on their own judgment. . . .

Perhaps most importantly, good learners do not *need* to have an absolute, final, irrevocable resolution to every problem. The sentence, "I don't know," does not depress them, and they certainly prefer it to the various forms of semantic nonsense that pass for "answers" to questions that do not as yet have any solution—or may never have one.[4]

Rick: I also know a number of people who disagree with part or all of that. Where do you readers stand? How about underlining in the quotation those aspects with which you agree and circling those with which you disagree?

You:

Barbara: Rick, how do you measure up as a learner, as Postman and Weingartner describe him?

Rick: Pretty good, I think. I love to get involved in problems and to experiment with ways of working them out. I also am terribly offended when other people try to give me answers. How do you readers measure yourselves?

[4] Neil Postman and Charles Weingartner, *Teaching as a Subversive Activity* (New York: Delacorte, 1969), pp. 31–33. Copyright © 1969, by Neil Postman and Charles Weingartner. Reprinted by permission of the publisher, Delacorte Press.

You:

Barbara: If good learners are important, we teachers ought to be concerned with encouraging the development of good-learner qualities in our students. What, specifically, can you readers do in your classrooms to help create good learners, either by this definition or your own?

You:

NEEDS ASSESSMENT

One of the greatest assets we can develop as teachers is the ability to deal with the causes of classroom problems rather than their symptoms. Let's look at the classic example of the student who needs a great deal of attention. Students like this are found in every grade and academic level. By the time these students reach junior-high nearly every teacher in the school system knows them by name. Once one of these students is in your room, he might demonstrate his need for attention by disrupting the class in any way he can, causing you a perplexing problem. Regardless of how you react to him, if you react at all you are probably rewarding him. To many people, negative attention is almost as reinforcing as positive attention; to a neglected child, punishment is better than nothing. On the other hand, by ignoring this student you may be increasing his need for attention, assuming you have the patience to put up with his antics in the first place. Sending him out of the room can alleviate the in-class pressure but will not solve the student's problem.

The dilemma is created in large part because you have been dealing with the symptoms rather than the cause of the problem. A more constructive approach would be to assess the student's need for attention and give it to him in positive ways, before he demonstrates disruptive behavior. For example, you might make special effort to greet him upon entering the classroom, solicit his opinion often during class, and in general show that you care about him.

Another problem is class boredom. If the students are bored or turned off to the presented materials, they may exhibit such symptoms as not turning in homework, not paying attention, fooling around with other students, or doing careless and uninspired assignments. By attacking these symptoms you can create a greater problem. Penalizing the students for disinterest, asking for even more homework, and giving low grades only causes alienation and breakdowns in communication. This problem can be better solved by attacking it at its roots. Work jointly with the students to diagnose the causes and change the material or its presentation accordingly.

"Needs Assessment" can help you develop the skill of assessing the needs of your class and dealing with these needs in an effective way. Because it is impossible to tell the difference between a cause and a symptom without having access to the actual situation, we cannot provide you with a list of causes and symptoms. The distinction between the two depends upon the situation. What may be a cause under one set of circumstances is a symptom in another. Therefore it is up to you, the teacher in the situation, to make this critical distinction and act accordingly. The following activity provides you with a framework for developing and practicing the skill of assessing needs.

Objectives

1. To differentiate between the causes and the symptoms of classroom problems.
2. To develop strategies for dealing effectively with the needs (causes) of your class.
3. To assess the success of your analysis and efforts.

Directions

Before teaching a lesson, sit down with your observer and outline some needs and demands of certain individuals and the total class that you expect during the upcoming lesson. When you have a list of six or more expectations, examine the list. Decide which you would like to fulfill and how you might fulfill them during the class. You might, for example, decide to pay special attention to one student by commenting on his clothing, asking his opinion about a book he is reading, and asking him to do an errand. Or you might determine that one student needs to have some time to be alone, and you could decide to satisfy his need by arranging with the librarian for him to spend some time alone in the library.

As the lesson progresses, the observer can watch specifically for the emergence of needs, check the accuracy of your predictions, and note whether or not individual needs are met. After the class you and your observer can meet and discuss the lesson, your predictions, and how well you met the prestated needs. The discussion can be based on the following questions.

Questions

1. How accurate were your predictions?
2. How well did you meet the predicted needs?
3. How did you meet needs other than those you predicted?
4. What significant need went unmet?
5. How can you satisfy that need the next time?
6. Were the needs causes or symptoms? How can you tell? If the need was a symptom, can you discover the underlying cause?

Follow-up

In the first part of this activity you looked at the immediate needs of an individual class. You can practice this activity until you feel you have some competence in determining and meeting the needs of your class. You might also begin to look at some long-range needs. Make a list of some long-range needs that you consider necessary for your class. Some examples are the troubled student who needs attention, bored students who need a change in class presentation (as cited above), a student who needs constant encouragement, a class that needs to develop trust and openness, a class that needs to learn how to communicate better with each other and the teacher, and students who need help to grasp the materials presented in class. Once you have listed at least six long-term needs, plan and try some procedures for fulfilling those needs.

SINGLE-STUDENT FOCUS

Our ability to see what's happening in our classroom is limited by the fact that we see the classroom only through our eyes. We can remember and even reexperience what schools and classrooms were like to us when we were children, but even these views are biased. We were future teachers and comprised a select population, one that most likely behaved and viewed school in relatively predictable ways. Not all of your students view the classroom in the same manner as you once did or do now. You can learn a great deal about the classroom environment by focusing on one student in the class and collecting detailed data concerning his actions and reactions, even if you cannot crawl inside his skin and experience the classroom exactly as he does. The following activity is designed to give you an opportunity to collect and analyze data concerning the behavior of a single student and to relate that data to your behavior as a teacher.

Objectives

1. To collect extensive data concerning the behavior of a single student.
2. To develop your awareness of the way in which one student acts and reacts in your classroom.
3. To analyze your teaching behavior in light of the effect it may have on a single student.
4. To compare the ways in which different students experience your classroom.

Directions

Together with your observer, select one of your students either because the student is worrisome to you, because he is especially responsive, because he is outstanding for another reason, or because he is especially typical of students in that class. The observer should then watch the behavior of that student carefully for a minimum of one hour.

The observer should take care to be unobtrusive, not to stare, or do anything to draw the attention of the student. Simply watch the student and unobtrusively take notes on his behavior during the observation period. It is difficult to be totally objective, but do your best to record observable behavior (he smiled) rather than your inferences about that behavior (he was happy). You can document that he smiled; you cannot know that he was happy (perhaps the smile was a grimace or a cover-up or was simply facetious). Use whatever shorthand techniques you can. The following is an example of a brief section of notes on a student's behavior:

> J. spent the first three minutes doodling, looking out the window, and shuffling papers. When a discussion about rockets began, he raised his hand and made a comment. The teacher nodded and said "Good," and Jim smiled. When the subject changed to pollution, he looked away from the teacher, shuffled papers, and began doodling. When called on he shrugged, mumbled "I don't know," and looked at the floor. . . .

Questions

Following the observation period, begin analyzing the notes. Circle behaviors that you consider positive and worth reinforcing; underline those that cause you some concern. Cross out any instances in which the observer's inferences found their way into the record (it happens easily). Structure your analysis around the following questions:

1. Look at your circles and underlinings. What do they tell you about the student's behavior?
2. Note instances in which there was some interaction between student and teacher. What do they tell you about the relationship between the two?
3. Note instances in which the student interacted with other students. What do these tell you about his relationship with other students?
4. What can you infer about the student's interest in subject matter?
5. How does the behavior of this student affect the teacher? The class as a whole?
6. As a result of this examination, what special needs of this student are apparent? What can you do to help meet his needs?
7. Are any changes in teacher behavior indicated? If so, what are they and how do you feel about them?

Follow-up

If as a result of this activity you are able to identify changes that you wish to make, you might find it meaningful to substantiate the effects of whatever changes you initiate. Allow some time for the changes to occur. Then repeat this activity, with the observer again focusing on the same student. Again analyze the observer's notes together, using the questions above and also comparing the two sets of notes. Were you able to initiate the desired changes? How effective were they in meeting the needs they were designed to meet? What implications does the comparison of the two sets of notes have for your future behavior as it affects this student?

You might also be interested in having the observer focus on a different student in the same class. You can then analyze the observer's notes concerning this second student's behavior. Compare your findings with the notes on the first student. What conclusions can you draw about the behavior of the two students? Do they relate to the teacher and to other students in similar ways? What implications do your observations have for your teaching?

Student Use

Because of the skill in objective observing and note-taking required for an activity of this type, it is probably not appropriate for students younger than high-school age. High-school students, however, could learn a great deal about their environments by using this technique, which has been adapted from a method used by cultural anthropologists to gather data (compare with "Shadowing," p. 80). Students might focus on the behavior of a speaker at an assembly, an individual in a court room (a judge, attorney, plaintiff, or defendant), or anyone they can observe unobtrusively. With the permission and cooperation of the subject, they might even record and analyze the behavior of a peer (perhaps in a group situation) or even a teacher. In these latter cases, however, they must be sure to work only with people who are willing to look objectively at their behavior. The most productive analyses will come from the observer and the observed analyzing the notes together. Therefore the permission and cooperation of the person to be observed must be secured prior to the observation period, and the privacy of the subject must be assured.

ACCEPTANCE

Recognizing and accepting the feelings behind a person's words and behavior is a difficult skill. It is certainly essential to a good relationship. Teachers more than anyone (expect perhaps parents) need to develop this skill. Often we evaluate and judge, but the very process of evaluating keeps us from understanding and accepting. When a child is acting sullen after a lost ballgame, we admonish him instead of recognizing his very real negative feelings. Rather than say "Stop slouching, Jim; look on the bright side," how much more understanding it would be to say "Jim, you seem very upset. I guess that game meant a lot to you." In the first instance, Jim will probably respond with hostility, if he responds at all. In the second instance, however, he will probably nod, immediately recognizing and responding to your understanding. Although we cannot change the situation, we have understood it.

Most of our responses to others' behavior can be classified as follows.

Acceptant. We recognize the feelings underlying the behavior. We convey that we understand and accept these feelings. In doing so, we neither encourage nor discourage the feelings (although we may express our personal response to the behavior—see "Sending I Messages" and "Self-Disclosure," p. 196 and p. 194).

Judgmental-positive. We judge the behavior to be good. We respond with an attempt to reinforce it. We may or may not recognize and understand the feelings that motivated the behavior.

Judgmental-negative. We judge the behavior to be undesirable. We respond with an attempt to change it. We probably do not recognize the feelings that motivated the behavior.

Although cultural influences have taught us to respond to others in judgmental ways, we believe that acceptant responses are almost always to be preferred. Only acceptant responses recognize that each individual must ultimately be responsible for himself. When we evaluate another's behavior, *even with a positive evaluation,* we are assuming responsibility for him and exercising control over him. When I say "That's excellent!," I'm implicitly reserving the right to also say "That's terrible!" In both instances I am probably attempting to control the person to whom I am responding, for I am judging him by some set of standards external to him.

We recognize, of course, that adults must at times exercise some control over children, but we maintain that these times are far less frequent than most adult behavior would seem to indicate. Acceptant, nonjudgmental responses, in which the other is granted the responsibility for his behavior that is rightfully his, facilitate the growth of responsible behavior. We encourage their use.

Note the difference between acceptant and judgmental responses in the following examples:

A third-grader comes in crying, proclaiming that "Johnny won't give me back my mitten."

Judgmental-positive. "You poor thing. I'll take care of it." (The child is likely to repeat the behavior, since he was rewarded for it. The teacher solves the problem.)

Judgmental-negative. "Oh, don't be a crybaby. You'll get it back." (The child's feelings are ignored, and the realationship between teacher and child is not enhanced. The problem remains.)

Acceptant. "You feel angry because you don't have your mitten. How might you get it?" (The child's feelings are recognized. He is encouraged to seek his own solution to the problem.)

A high-school junior proudly shows off the motorcycle he bought with money he earned.

Judgmental-positive. "How great. That's a beautiful bike."

Judgmental-negative. "Why did you waste your money on that?"

Acceptant. "You must be very proud of saving enough money to buy that by yourself."

A junior-high student slams into your room, throws down his books, and tells you how unfair Mr. _____ is for reprimanding him.

Judgmental-positive. "That's OK. When you have problems with him, just come in here."

Judgmental-negative. "Well, if you acted as ugly with him as you are right now, I don't blame him. Sit down."

Acceptant. "You're very upset because Mr. _____ scolded you. Let's talk about it."

A student hands you a bedraggled-looking assignment, sheepishly explaining that she dropped it in a puddle on the way to school.

Judgmental-positive. "That's OK. I'm sure it wasn't your fault."

Judgmental-negative. "That looks awful. You should know better than to try to turn it in that way."

Acceptant. "I can see that you're embarrassed about it. What would you like to do now?"

Objectives

1. To distinguish between judgmental and acceptant responses.
2. To identify judgmental and acceptant responses in your verbal classroom behavior.
3. To use acceptant responses.

Directions

A. Alone, with your observer, or in your support group, practice making acceptant responses to the following situations. Use each other to get feedback on whether your responses are acceptant or judgmental.

1. A child of middle-elementary age refuses to work with another child, saying that "He keeps picking on me."

2. A high-school student tells you he's thinking of dropping out of school.

3. A colleague tearfully tells you that she expects to be fired.

4. During your conference with her, a fourteen-year-old stares at the floor when you ask her why she hasn't been participating.

B. You and your support group can set up mini-role-playing situations for each other to practice making nonjudgmental, acceptant responses. Think of individual situations like those above and role-play the individuals involved.

C. In your classroom use a tape recorder or have your observer record every personal response you make to students. Record on the accompanying worksheet each response from the tape or the observer's notes. Then classify each response as judgmental-positive, judgmental-negative, or acceptant.

Questions

1. In which category did most of your responses fall?

2. Combining the first two categories, did you make more judgmental or more acceptant responses?

3. Is it easier for you to make one kind of response than another? What does that mean to you?

4. Find one response that you are especially pleased to have made. What was the effect (or probable effect) of that response on the student? (You might ask the student for his reaction to it.)

5. Find one response that could have been better. What was the effect (or probable effect) of that response on the student? (Again, you might ask the student for feedback.) How could you have responded differently?

6. Are you satisfied with the data before you? Why or why not?

Follow-up

As with other activities in which you collect data concerning your classroom behavior, significant changes occur only over time. Daily and weekly analyses, with comparisons drawn and trends noted, are essential if you are serious about changing any aspect of your behavior. We therefore recommend that you repeat this activity as you feel it necessary.

Monitoring your verbal acceptance of behavior may also be helpful in situations in which you and a particular student are having difficulty in your relationship with each other. If you have such a student, an ob-

Worksheet

Acceptance

Response	Judgmental-positive	Judgmental-negative	Acceptant

server might record every response you make to him over a significant period of time (four hours or more spread out as is convenient for you and the observer). You can then classify those responses and draw the implications.

Student Use

Students of all ages can be made aware of the difference between judgment and acceptance, for all students have been exposed to both and have reacted to both. Your classroom might become the place where judgmental and acceptant behaviors are analyzed. Ask students how they feel when another person says, either explicitly or implicitly, "You are bad," and how they feel when another person says "I understand . . ." To illustrate the difference between judgment and acceptance, use examples that are appropriate to the age and maturity of your students. Then draw from the students a long list of statements that belong in each category. You might post these on a bulletin board and ask students to help one another increase the proportion of acceptant remarks in your classroom.

TEACHER WALKING MAP

The way a teacher moves about the classroom has a profound effect on the messages he conveys to students, on the ways in which he relates to students, and ultimately on the learning that occurs. His movement demonstrates how he feels *about* students; at the same time it has a determining effect on his relationships *with* students. For example, a teacher who always sits or stands behind a desk puts a physical barrier between himself and his students. If he remains behind the desk because he feels uncomfortable relating closely to students, the students will probably perceive him as being emotionally as well as physically distant. The students are not likely to attempt to relate more closely with him, so the emotional distance is thereby increased. Thus the very action of remaining behind a desk (which may not have been the result of a conscious choice on the part of the teacher) reinforces the original feeling that motivated the action. Even if the teacher is aware of the emotional distance between himself and his students, he is unlikely to bridge that distance until he realizes how his physical deportment is contributing to it.

Let's look at another example: If a generally active teacher who moves throughout the classroom consistently avoids one corner, it may be because a student in that corner makes the teacher uncomfortable. By avoiding that corner the teacher conveniently avoids the student, while at the same time creating even greater distance from that student. Until the teacher becomes aware of his pattern of movement, he is unlikely to confront and change his feelings of discomfort.

Objectives

1. To help you monitor your movement in a classroom.
2. To help you identify the possible effects of your classroom movement on students.
3. To assist you in making your physical movement contribute to your goals.

Directions

For a specified period of time (perhaps one period or one hour) a colleague observer can map on paper your movement about the classroom. The observer can use the following directions:

1. Draw a map of the classroom, including the furniture arrangement.
2. Chart with a pencil the teacher's location at the beginning of class, and follow his movement throughout the agreed-upon time period.
3. Consecutively number spots at which the teacher stops.
4. Draw concentric circles around spots where the teacher remains for significant time periods: one circle for every three minutes.

For example, a map of a traditional classroom with a teacher who spends most of his time in front might look something like the one on p. 177.

Questions

1. In which areas of your classroom did you spend most of your time?
2. Did you neglect any area(s)?
3. Did the students' activities determine your movements in any way? How?
4. What effect did the seating arrangement have on your movements?
5. What effect might your movement have had on students?
6. Do you want to make any changes, based on the information you now have? Why or why not?

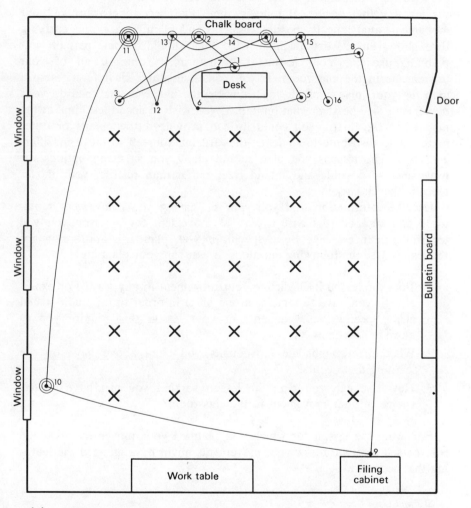

Chalk board

Desk

Door

Window

Window

Window

Bulletin board

Work table

Filing cabinet

X = Student locations

Follow-up

A teacher's movement in the classroom can have a significant effect on the learning that occurs. If follows, then, that becoming aware of your movement, analyzing its possible effects, and planning for and carrying through movements that facilitate your goals should become part of your planning process. Your lessons may determine some or all of your movements in the classroom. If you consistently include references to a map in your plans, or if you consistently use the chalkboard, your movements will be somewhat limited. If you wish to spend less time at the map or at the board, you could instead provide dittoed maps or other materials to distribute to students, thus freeing yourself to move in different ways. The lessons you plan should allow you as many options for movement as possible and should free, rather than restrict, your movement in the classroom.

Use the information that you gain by having your movement monitored and mapped to devise a plan of movement for a lesson you will use in the next few days. Be as specific in your plan as is appropriate for the lesson. Use the following questions to assist in your planning:

1. Does the lesson itself dictate your movement in any way? For example, do you have to remain in one place in order to use audio-visual aids? Specify those elements of your lesson that require you to move in specific ways.
2. What effect might the movements you cited above have on the learning that occurs?
3. How else can you plan the lesson so that you can have greater choice of your movement in the classroom?

Following the lesson for which you planned your movement, evaluate for yourself afterward how your movements might have affected the learning that occurred.

Student Use

Like the teacher in the classroom, everyone's movements are determined to some extent by his significant relationships with people and by his interests and concerns. At the same time, one's movements contribute to one's relationships and interests. At home we may spend much time in one room because that room offers stimulating activities or because a particular person is often there. Students of middle-elementary age and

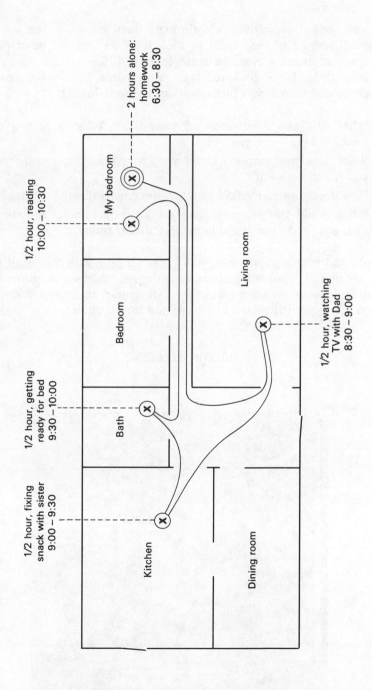

2 hours alone:
homework
6:30 – 8:30

My bedroom

1/2 hour, reading
10:00 – 10:30

Bedroom

Living room

1/2 hour, getting
ready for bed
9:30 – 10:00

Bath

1/2 hour, watching
TV with Dad
8:30 – 9:00

1/2 hour, fixing
snack with sister
9:00 – 9:30

Kitchen

Dining room

older can map their movements through their homes in an evening, noting the amount of time spent in each location and the other people present at that location. Note the example on p. 179.

After students have monitored their movements, you might structure small group discussions with such questions as the following:

1. Where did you spend most of your time? What were you doing there? Whom were you with?
2. What does your map say about you, your interests, and the people you spend time with?
3. How does your map reflect your feelings concerning the evening?
4. What would you like your map for a future evening to look like? Plan one for an evening at home in the near future.

If you and your students wish, you might set up a gallery of your maps of an evening at home using either rough maps, redrawn maps, or maps for future or ideal evenings. Remember, of course, that any student who chooses not to participate must be respected for his choice.

BULLETIN BOARDS

Location	Contents	*T/S*	*Sa/C*	*Cen/Un*	*d/in/is*	*M/Tr*

Bulletin boards in schools and classrooms can be very revealing about life in a school or classroom. Use the accompanying worksheet to inventory the bulletin boards in your school.

Take a close look at six or more bulletin boards in your school (the more the better). Indicate in the Location column where the board is: entrance hall, Miss Allison's first-grade classroom, west wall of cafeteria, whatever. Then in the Contents column briefly describe the board: announcements (include dates) and personal notes, a phonics circus wagon with initial letters, a Christmas scene. Then code the contents, using the following categories and any others you consider important.

In the first coding column place a *T* next to those bulletin boards that are obviously teacher designed, an *S* next to those in which students apparently had contributed significantly to the design. In the second column use an *Sa* to indicate those that are safe and noncontroversial, a *C* for those that may be controversial (for example, a springtime basket of flowers is probably safe, but an article about how a local manufacturer's waste-disposal practices are killing local vegetation is probably controversial). In the third column use *Cen* if it appears that a teacher may have censored or regulated the contents of the bulletin board, *Un* if you think the students were allowed to post whatever they chose. In the fourth column indicate whether the contents are decorative (*d*), informational (*in*), or issue-oriented (*is*). In the fifth column indicate with *M* or *Tr* whether you think the bulletin board is meaningful or trivial. Use the remaining columns to code the boards according to self-made categories that emerge as you review the information on your worksheet.

After completing the worksheet, answer the following questions:

1. Are the bulletin boards you saw basically similar or quite different from one another? What factors do you think account for their similarities and/or differences?
2. Do the bulletin boards in your school serve students well? Explain.
3. If (or when) you have a bulletin board at your disposal, how can you best use it? Who should determine its contents? What functions should it serve?

LOG CONVERSATION: LEARNING DETAILS

Rick: With all the talk these days about the irrelevancy of examinations, I looked up again what Alfred North Whitehead said about remembering details.

Whatever be the detail with which you cram your student, the chance of his meeting in after-life exactly that detail is almost infinitesimal; and if he does meet it, he will probably have forgotten what you taught him about it. The really useful training yields a comprehension of a few general principles with a thorough grounding in the way they apply to a variety of concrete details. In subsequent practice the men will have forgotten your particular details; but they will remember by an unconscious common sense how to apply principles to immediate circumstances. Your learning is useless to you till you have lost your text-books, burnt your lecture notes, and forgotten the minutiae which you learnt by heart for the examination. What, in the way of detail, you continually require will stick in your memory as obvious facts like the sun and moon; and what you casually require can be looked up in any work of reference.[5]

Barbara: That statement is really meaningful for me because I recall very little of the details I crammed into my head in all those night-before-the-exam sessions. But lots of people think that learning details is very important. What do you readers think? Is it necessary to learn details that will be forgotten in either the near or the distant future?

You:

Rick: I also believe that learning details is unimportant. I believe that in my classroom we must emphasize concepts rather than details. That's hard to implement, though, since the details often seem essential to understanding the concept. One way I get around this problem is to let the students supply the details for the concept. That way it's their experience rather than mine that is significant. How do you readers implement your position on learning details in the classroom?

You:

LESSON-ANALYSIS CONTINUUM

Your personal analysis of your teaching self is by far the most meaningful analysis, and your most useful analyses are the ones that can

[5] Alfred North Whitehead, *The Aims of Education and Other Essays* (New York: Macmillan, 1929; Mentor, 1961, p. 37). Copyright renewed 1957 by Evelyn Whitehead.

easily be translated into specific directions. Lesson-analysis continua are useful tools in generating specific steps for you to use to improve your teaching. Use these continua at regular intervals to generate a continuous flow of relevant data about your teaching, which in turn sustains a constant growth as a teacher. If you wish, use an observer to verify your perceptions of your teaching. This is not necessary, however, because lesson-analysis continua can be used efficiently on your own.

Objective

To generate specific steps for the improvement of your teaching.

Directions

As soon after teaching a lesson as possible fill in the accompanying worksheet as follows (see the model worksheet filled out as an example).

1. Find the spot on the continuum that best describes your feelings of how well the lesson went. A zero means that it went as badly as possible: you did not accomplish what you set out to do, and you are very uncomfortable with the way you handled situations as they came up. An eight means that it went as perfectly as possible: you accomplished what you set out to accomplish and you feel very good about the whole lesson. You are not allowed to rate the lesson exactly in the middle; therefore, no four is on the continuum. In rating, keep in mind your goals and how successfully they were accomplished.

2. List in question one all the factors that contributed to your rating the lesson as high as you did. If you rated your lesson a five, why wasn't it a three, a two, or a one? Make this list as complete as possible. When you feel you have run out of factors, try to add two more.

3. List in question two all the factors that you think might have made the lesson better. To insure that the sentences are in a form that can easily be translated into action, start each item on this list with "I will . . ." Check this list for completeness by asking yourself "Would this lesson now be as perfect as possible?" Keep adding to your list until you can answer that question affirmatively.

4. Rank the items on both your lists according to their potential importance in accomplishing your goals, putting a 1 after the most important item, and so on.

5. On the bottom of the worksheet write four self-contracts, two as a result of your responses to the first question, and two as a result of

Date: February 6; Class: History—Celebration of Massachusetts being admitted
to the Union on this day in 1788.

worst
possible
lesson   perfect
                                               lesson

    0   1   2   3   5   6   7   8

1: What factors contributed to your rating this lesson as high as you did?

(1). I asked a lot of class-five questions (see "What Kind of Questions Do
You Ask?," p. 199).   1

(2). I was prepared.   4

(3). I had mimeographed material to give out.   5

(4). I called on every member of the class at least once.   2

(5). I moved about the room as I had planned, making physical contact
with those students whom I often avoid.   3

2. What will you do to make it a perfect lesson?

(1). I will be more humorous (lesson was too dry).   4

(2). I will let a student speak longer when he is interested in a topic.   1

(3). I will loosen my collar so I will not be uncomfortable.   5

(4). I will try to find more personal meanings for the students in the material.   3

(5). I will listen better to the students' responses and not rehearse my next
comments.   2

3. Self-contracts

(1). I will continue to ask a lot of class-five questions.

(2). I will continue to call on every member of the class.

(3). I will be sure to let each student speak until he is finished.

(4). I will listen to student comments without rehearsing my next comments.

Worksheet   **Lesson Analysis**

Date: **Class:**

worst
possible _____ perfect
lesson   0   1   2   3   5   6   7   8 lesson

1. What factors contributed to your rating this lesson as high as you did?

2. What would you have to do to make it a perfect lesson?

3. Self-contracts

your responses to the second question. Begin each of your self-contracts with "I will . . ." The next time that you teach a similar lesson, refer to your self-contracts.

If you wish to use an observer, have him simultaneously but separately fill out a worksheet. Then compare your perceptions with his and discuss any discrepancies.

Follow-up

Repeat this activity at least once a week for a period of six-to-eight weeks. See what patterns emerge. It is an indication of progress if the answers to question two on your worksheets are gradually becoming answers to question one. If you are having trouble improving your instruction, perhaps your items are not specific enough. A common problem is that the items are too vague to be specific steps for improvement.

HOW DID IT GO?

Often it is helpful to review a completed lesson by answering a series of questions (see accompanying worksheet) to increase your awareness of yourself and the class. By answering such questions on a regular basis (at least once a week), you will generate enough data to be able to differentiate the random actions and the patterns in your behavior. By reviewing your patterns, you can begin to find areas in your teaching that might become entry points for trying new behavior.

"How Did It Go?" can also be a diagnostic instrument for discovering more specific problems. You might find that a specific concern uncovered here can be amplified by other activities in this book. For example, you might find in "How Did It Go?" that your classroom movement is an area of concern, so you refer to such activities as "Teacher-Walking Map," "Seating Arrangement," or "Body Language." Or perhaps you find that generating class discussions is an area of concern, so you might refer to "What Kind of Questions Do You Ask?," "Responses to Student Responses," or "Single-Student Focus."

Objectives

1. To gather continuous data on a weekly basis about your teaching.
2. To find patterns that emerge from this data about your teaching.
3. To examine your patterns for possible behavior changes.

The questions below are designed to help you keep a record of the activities in your classes, your feelings and insights, and any changes you observe in yourself or others. You can organize and bring meaning to your teaching experience by reflecting on the kinds of questions below. You might also become aware of feelings or patterns of behavior that you had not previously noted.

Record your feelings, insights, and observations after selected classes. Use the following questions as a guide: answer one, or all, or other self-made questions that are more appropriate for your situation.

Date_____ Class_____

1. What happened during the class? (Briefly outline to help yourself recall events).

2. How did you feel about yourself in today's class?

3. What did you like about the class? Students? Yourself?

4. What did you dislike about the class? Students? Yourself?

5. How did you react to students' talk in today's class?

6. How did students react to you?

7. What was your greatest strength in this class? Weakness?

8. Did you notice any changes in the class from former sessions? Changes in students? Changes in yourself?

Directions

Fill out the accompanying worksheet on a weekly basis by answering the questions after teaching a class. After you have collected at least five worksheets, begin to look for different patterns in your teaching. In looking for patterns, notice recurring items or themes that are woven into nearly every worksheet. Try to imagine that you are a detective fitting the pieces of a mystery together. Throw out the irrelevant and concentrate on the central; however, be careful not to eliminate an important clue because it seems meaningless. Like a detective, carefully consider evidence before discarding it. Once you have found the significant aspects of your worksheets, see what implications are there for you. Try to identify areas of your teaching that you might like to modify or analyze, and make a list of them.

Follow-up

From the list you generated, start with the concern that is most important for you and use other activities in this book to help you diagnose the nature of that concern in more detail. You may also use a colleague or observer to help with your diagnosis. Once you begin to understand more clearly the nature of your concern, experiment with new behaviors. (You may find it useful to repeat "How Did It Go?" at a later time to see how well your experiment is working.) Eventually select another concern from your list and repeat.

SHOWCASE LESSON

After you have taken a close, scrutinizing look at some of the lessons you have taught (by using such devices as the "Lesson-Analysis Continuum," p. 183, and "How Did It Go?" p. 187), you might find it helpful to design what for you would be a "showcase lesson," a lesson that you would be proud to display as an example of what you can do as a teacher. You will probably find, as you describe all the elements that constitute a total showcase lesson, that you, as one individual, cannot control all of them. You will find, however, that you can control many of the elements. We believe that acknowledging your power and identifying the areas in which you have power can give you greater control over your teaching.

1. If you were to teach a showcase lesson, where would you teach it? Describe the location.

2. To whom would you teach it? Describe the students (attitude, dress, relationships to each other and to you, manner of response and interactions, preparation, seating, and other important factors).

3. Why would you teach it? Describe yourself as the teacher (attitude, dress, approach, relationships with students, preparation, and any other important personal factors).

4. Do you have a particular subject in mind? If so, what would the lesson be about?

5. Describe the lesson.

6. Describe any other important factors, such as weather and materials, not listed above.

Worksheet 2

A. I have control over—   B. I cannot control—

Objectives

1. To be aware of all the elements that influence your success as a teacher.
2. To differentiate between those factors over which you have control and those over which you do not have control.
3. To act to control those elements which you can control, and to make your peace with those you cannot.

Directions

Fill in Worksheet 1 to describe what for you would be a showcase lesson (an eight on the lesson-analysis continuum, p. 183).

Then turn to Worksheet 2 and list each factor mentioned on Worksheet 1 in either Column A to indicate that you feel in control of it, or Column B to indicate that you feel powerless to control it. Some may be difficult to classify, but do so anyway.

Questions

1. Look carefully at the factors you included in each category on Worksheet 2. Do those in Column A have something in common? Those in Column B? What differences exist between those in Column A and those in Column B?
2. Circle every factor on Worksheet 2 that is absolutely essential to a successful lesson for you. How much control do you have over the really important factors?
3. Which of the really important factors that are within your control (those you circled in Column A) have you made sure occurred in your teaching of the last few days? Which will you be sure to include tomorrow?
4. Who would you want to have see your showcase lesson? Is your ideal consistent with that of your administrators? colleagues? students? parents? school board? Do they limit you? What can you do about it?

Follow-up

Plan your next day's or week's activities with this analysis in mind. Include all the factors of your showcase lesson that you can control and make whatever attempts you can to move some factors from Column B into Column A. After teaching, analyze your lesson. How well did it meet the criteria you set up for yourself on Worksheet 1?

Student Use

This activity, as it stands, can be used to obtain important feedback from your students (junior-high age or older). Simply rewrite Worksheet 1 to obtain the student point of view. After they complete the worksheets, use small groups to discuss the findings. Be sure to share your conception of the ideal lesson. Use their input to design lessons that will provide growth and learning for everyone.

In addition, older students might be interested in designing a showcase club meeting, a showcase date, or a showcase family dinner. Design appropriate questions for Worksheet 1 (ask them to help supply the questions) and use Worksheet 2 for them to differentiate those factors they feel in control of and those they do not. What they will usually discover is that they can control only themselves and their behavior, and not the behavior of others. This, of course, is an important discovery, one that you will probably find of vital interest for discussion. You can help them, and they can help each other, to take control of those elements they can control and to reconcile themselves to those they cannot.

TIME ANALYSIS

In the final analysis, each of us most clearly expresses ourself in our behavior. What we *do* is the strongest and clearest indication of what we value.

Most of the school day we are involved with children. Many of us find ourselves whisked through the day intervening in crises, solving unpredicted problems, and responding to old and new needs. But each of us also has some time—before school, during lunch, during quiet periods and lulls, or after school—when we are somewhat more in control of what we do. This brief activity is designed to help you look at how you spend the precious moments you have to yourself as a teacher.

Below are listed a number of activities. Reflect on the way you have spent your probably very limited "free time" in school in the past week. Indicate next to each activity your estimate of how much time in the last week you spent engaged in that activity between 7:00 A.M. and

5:00 P.M. (a fair estimate, we think, of a teacher's day). At the end are some blank lines for you to fill in other activities that we missed.

_____talk with teacher(s)   _____investigate com-
_____talk with administrator(s)   munity resources
_____talk with student(s)   _____work with extra-
_____run an errand   curricular activity
_____plan a lesson   _____eat
_____read a book   _____in-service work
_____write (anything)   _____
_____make a grocery list   _____
    or do a home chore   _____
_____work in *Discovering*   _____
    Your Teaching Self   _____
_____sleep or rest   _____

Look over your list. What does it tell you about how you spend your precious moments to yourself? How do the activities you engaged in serve you? Would you like to use any time differently? How? What will you do?

SELF-DISCLOSURE

The JoHari Window (named after its originators, Joe Luft and Harry Ingham) represents the processes of self-disclosure and feedback.[6]

	Known to self	Not known to self
Known to others	A. What both you and I know about me	B. What you know about me that I don't know
Not known to others	C. What I know about me that you don't know	D. What neither of us knows

The chart represents everything about an individual. Section A represents all those things about me that I have shared with you—my public self. Section B represents those things about me of which you are aware but

[6] Joseph Luft and Harry Ingham, "The JoHari Window, a Graphic Model of Interpersonal Awareness," in *Proceedings of the Western Training Laboratory in Group Development* (Los Angeles: University of California Extension Office, August 1955). See also, Joseph Luft, *Group Processes: An Introduction to Group Dynamics,* 2nd ed. (Palo Alto, California: National Press Books, 1970).

I am not, my blind spots (perhaps my zipper is open); or, on a more crucial level, perhaps I am motivated by unconscious needs. Section C contains those things I have kept from you, my very private self. Section D represents those things about me that neither of us know.

As I disclose more of myself to you, Area A extends into Area C. As you give me feedback about myself, Area A extends into Area B.

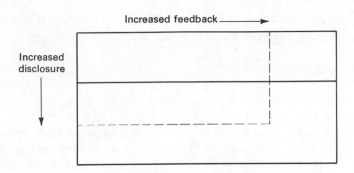

Thus Area A becomes increasingly larger and I become both more open and public and more aware of myself.

Open, aware people tend to facilitate openness and awareness in others too. Therefore it seems reasonable to suggest that teachers who disclose themselves to their students will be more likely to facilitate students' self-disclosure, thereby developing relationships characterized by openness and honesty, qualities essential to effective communication and trust.

How do you act with your students? Are your relationships with them characterized by openness and self-disclosure, or are you closed, private, and distant? The following activity is designed to help you find out.

Objectives

1. To monitor your teaching to see how much you disclose about yourself.
2. To self-disclose in a different pattern if it is appropriate.

Directions

On at least two different occasions, preferably one in which you expect to feel comfortable with students and one in which you expect some discomfort, have an observer record every statement you make for a period of at least fifteen minutes. Later, carefully examine the two transcripts. Mark every instance in which you actually shared something of your personal self with your students.

Questions

1. Were your expectations realistic? Were you comfortable in one situation and uncomfortable in the other, as you expected to be?
2. Can you see any differences in your verbal behavior in the two situations?
3. Does your verbal behavior have any relationship to your comfort?
4. Is there anything you noted that you would like to change?

Follow-up

If you have found that you do not self-disclose enough in your class, you may wish to begin to change that pattern. One way to tell if you need to self-disclose more is to use the student-feedback form (provided) to see how much your students know about you. How much or little they know about you will substantiate your interpretation of the data collected in this activity. Should you decide to opt for more self-disclosure, begin with small, personal things, such as preferences, anecdotes that relate to your lesson, or worries and concerns you might have in common with your students. Avoid using self-disclosure as a means of moralizing, for you will only defeat your purpose ("When I was your age, I was never lazy"). Encourage your students to disclose as well. Soon you may find that your class has a much more intimate and exciting environment where meaningful dialogue is the rule rather than the exception.

SENDING "I MESSAGES"

Meaningful communication between people (the communication between adults and children is of special interest to us) often breaks down because one party (or both) continually tells the other what's wrong with him rather than identifying how he himself is feeling in the situation. When I tell someone what's wrong with him, I virtually take away from him all responsibility for himself. Since I know what is wrong, I also know how to "correct" it. Thus I leave him powerless and probably defensive.

Thomas Gordon calls these ineffective, damaging messages "YOU messages," while terming the effective messages "I messages." [7] YOU messages, in addition to denying the other's responsibility for himself, may

[7] Thomas Gordon, M.D., *Parent Effectiveness* (New York: Peter H. Wyden, 1970).

also be projections on the part of the speaker: YOU messages may be blaming the other for faults the speaker feels in himself. He may also be denying the other's internal reality by completely failing to understand or empathize with him, or he may be ignoring his own feelings. He may also be so far removed from understanding himself that he is not even aware of his own feelings. YOU messages are those that explicitly or implicitly *blame* (you are naughty; you should know better; you didn't understand; you are wrong), that *direct* (you go outside; you clean up this mess), that *threaten* (if you don't, . .). I messages, on the other hand, share personal feelings (I really get upset when there is fighting near me; I'm angry; I'm very nervous because I see the possibility of Jimmy's glasses being broken).

I messages, in which the sender states facts about his feelings in the situation but does not tell others what they should do, refrain from blaming, directing, threatening, or preaching. They reveal, and since they do, they facilitate rather than hinder communication (see also "Self-Disclosure," p. 194).

YOU messages, on the other hand, facilitate only conflict. Think back to the last time someone blamed, directed, or threatened you. Perhaps you recently heard "Why didn't you . . ?" or "Would you *please* . . !" or "If you don't . . !" How did you feel in that situation? Did you feel accepted or rejected? worthy or unworthy? responsive or unresponsive? How did you communicate back? What did that encounter do to your relationship with the other individual involved?

Imagine the following situations:

1. In a fifth-grade classroom, Scott knocks his books off the desk. The teacher responds, "Scott, you pick up those books this instant! There will be no such naughty behavior in this classroom!" How do you imagine Scott feels after this YOU message? What effect on the relationship between Scott and his teacher might this exchange have?

2. Now imagine a similar classroom. Johnny knocks his books off his desk. The teacher responds. "Oh! Loud noises like that really frighten me!" How might Johnny feel after this I message? What effect might this exchange have on the relationship between Johnny and his teacher?

The following provide further examples of YOU and I messages:

3. During a student presentation, two students are holding a private conversation in the corner, obviously ignoring the speaker.

YOU-message response by teacher: "Pay attention to the speaker. Rudeness is not acceptable behavior."
I-message response by teacher: "It really makes me feel frustrated and worthless when my audience ignores me. I assume that our speaker feels the same way. Do you feel that way?"

4. In a kindergarten room, two children get into a fight. When she intervenes, the teacher is punched.
YOU-message response by teacher: "You unruly girl! It's not nice to punch!"
I-message response by teacher: "Ouch! It hurts me to be punched!"

In each of the situations above, the YOU message tells the child he is bad, a message he will probably resist or perhaps ignore. The I message, however, conveys only the teacher's feelings. It allows the child to maintain his self-respect, his personal frame of reference, and responsibility for his behavior. He is made aware of the consequences of his behavior without being made to feel guilty, ashamed, or rebellious.

Of course, every teacher must at times control a child's behavior, but these times are probably far less frequent than we think. We can help children grow immensely in their ability to control their behavior, and in their ability to trust themselves, by refraining from YOU messages, which deny them responsibility and self-confidence. Use I messages, which accept them as they are while teaching them self-respect and responsibility for themselves.

Objectives

1. To distinguish between YOU messages and I messages.
2. To identify YOU messages and I messages in your classroom talk.
3. To link student responses to the type of messages you send.
4. To increase your use of I messages.

Directions

Before analyzing your verbal behavior, check your understanding of the difference between YOU messages and I messages by classifying each of the statements below. If the message blames, threatens, or warns, regardless of the words used, it is a YOU message. "I'm upset because you're so naughty" is really a YOU message in disguise because emphasis is on the blame rather than the feelings of the sender. (Answers appear after the "Follow-up" part of this section).

1. "Pick up your room or you'll go to bed early."
2. "It's not nice to speak out of turn."

3. "The hair on my arms stands on end when you shout like that."
4. "Do you enjoy making me angry?"
5. "You're just trying to get my goat, aren't you?"
6. "I am becoming more and more aggravated by your tone of voice."
7. "I'm very tired and just can't take extra noise right now."
8. "Stop that yelling! You're bothering me."

Ask your observer to record all the messages you send to students in your classroom in response to their behavior during a specified period of time (half-hour minimum). The observer should include some indication of their response to your message, or you can mechanically record a half-hour segment of your class and later select a series of your messages. Afterward, classify each message as either an I message or a YOU message.

Questions

1. Did you send a preponderance of one type of message? Which type?
2. What effect did each YOU message have?
3. What effect did each I message have?
4. Are you satisfied with the messages you sent? Can you identify one message that could have been better?

Follow-up

As with other activities in which you examine your behavior in the classroom, the significance of this activity is related to your commitment to continual self-evaluation. We recommend that you repeat your analysis at regular intervals. If you wish, compare the kind of messages you send at one time of day with those you send at another time. You can trace your progress by repeating an activity regularly over a significant period of time and comparing later findings with earlier ones. The emphasis is always on your progress toward achieving specified goals.

Answers: 1. YOU; 2. YOU; 3. I; 4. YOU; 5. YOU; 6. I; 7. I; 8. YOU.

WHAT KINDS OF QUESTIONS DO YOU ASK?

Traditionally, one of the primary duties of a teacher has been to ask questions. We are all familiar with the image of a classroom filled with rows of desks facing forward. Each is occupied by a student who is expected to respond positively (often by waving his hand to indicate his ability to answer) to the teacher, who stands facing the children and asking them questions. The questions frequently have one "right" answer which the teacher knows, and the children are to demonstrate that they know it too.

William Glasser interviewed a class of fourth-graders about questions and "right" answers.

I started the discussion with the question, "What do teachers want from children in school?" After some initial hesitation, the group responded that teachers want children to learn, to do well, to get good grades, and to go on to college. The children were repeating all the cliché answers that they had heard from their parents and their teachers for so long. As I stated my questions more clearly, however, asking what the teachers want from children every day, they said that the teachers want answers. In response to, "Answers to what?" the children said answers, both oral and written, to all kinds of questions that teachers pose. Because I was pursuing a particular course, I asked the children to discuss the kinds of answers teachers wanted. Did the teachers want any particular kind of answer? After a few hesitations and a few false starts, one of the children answered, "Yes, what the teacher wants is right answers." When I followed with, "Do you mean that the questions asked are questions that can be answered by a right answer?" there was general agreement that they were. I then asked them, "Can teachers ask questions that do not have right and wrong answers but that still can have important answers?" This question threw the students completely off balance and they were unable to recover for the rest of the discussion. Despite much talk, no satisfactory response emerged. Because I was in a teaching situation and because we were in school, the students' orientation was almost totally to right and wrong answers. One boy, however, said, "Do you mean questions we give our opinion on?" When I asked him to continue, he said, "Well, do teachers ever ask questions that call for the opinions of the students in the class?" He thought for a while, and the others thought for a while, and they decided that what they thought—their opinions, their ideas, their judgments, and their observations—was rarely asked for in class.[8]

Although we have been moving away from the kind of classroom and interaction described above, the significance of the questioning patterns of the teacher has certainly not been lessened. It may be that the questions asked by the more open, innovative teacher are even more significant, though probably of a different nature, than those asked by the more conventional teacher. Whereas most of the conventional teacher's questions are probably directed toward large groups and usually require factual in-

[8] William Glasser, *Schools Without Failure* (New York: Harper & Row, 1969), p. 51.

formation for answers, the teacher in a more open situation generally relies more heavily on questions directed to individuals, questions with no "right" answers that elicit individual opinions and concerns instead. This is not to say, of course, that each teacher uses only one type of question, but simply that a teacher's purposes and ideas, including the atmosphere he has established in the classroom, significantly affect the kinds of questions he asks. Some questions demand single, factual answers, others require that students look for relationships and concepts, and still others require opinions and personal responses. Each has its place in the classroom and each serves a different purpose. The competent, flexible teacher must be aware of the types of questions and of his use of them.

Once you know the types and the probable effects of your use of each type, you can consciously select the questions you need in a given situation to elicit the kind of response you want. If you want to promote active thought and discussion, you probably will not choose to ask a question with one right answer; conversely, if you want to elicit information, you will not ask a question that can be answered with a student's opinion.

The five examples below demonstrate five possible categories of questions.

Class 1: Questions to which students can respond with a yes or no answer.

Example: "Was George Washington the first president of the United States?"

Class 2: Questions that students can answer with a simple, short, factual answer.

Example: "Who was the first president of the United States?"

Class 3: Questions that require students to do some immediate thinking to find a correct answer (there is a correct answer).

Examples: "What are the subject and the object in the preceding sentence?" "What is the sum of 20, 89, and 34?"

Class 4: Questions that require students to look for relationships and underlying concepts. There might be many acceptable responses.

Example: "What similarities do you find between the causes of the First and Second World Wars?"

Class 5: Questions that ask for divergent thinking, including personal opinions and responses, and solutions to hypothetical situations for which there are no "correct" answers. Any response is acceptable.

Examples: "What do you consider to be more worthy of your concern, earth ecology or space exploration?" "What would happen if, as of next week, there were no laws?"

Objectives

1. To increase your awareness of the kinds of questions that you can ask.

2. To identify your questioning patterns.
3. To relate the kinds of questions you ask to classroom activities.

Directions

Have an observer record verbatim every question you ask in class in a specified period of time (fifteen minutes as a minimum), or use an audio- or video-recorder and later select the questions from the tape. Then classify each question according to the five categories described above. Tally your classifications on the accompanying worksheet.

Questions

1. What kinds of questions did you ask most often?
2. What effect did each of these questions have on what went on in your classroom?
3. In looking over the questions you asked, which do you especially like?
4. What do you see that you would like to change? What will you do to effect the change?

Follow-up

You have now seen and examined your questions during one short segment of your classroom behavior, a segment that may or may not have been typical. To understand more fully how your questions affect your classroom, repeat the activity. You might record a longer segment, or a number of short segments either taken at different times during a relatively short overall time period (one or two days) or taken at the same hour on consecutive days or weeks. Recording and analyzing a number of segments at different times will allow you to compare your questioning behavior at different times of day (and perhaps with different youngsters). Recording at the same hour daily or weekly will make it easier to identify any changes that gradually occur.

In either case, ask yourself:

1. What similarities exist in my questioning style during each recording? What do these mean?
2. What differences exist? What do these mean?
3. What effect did my kinds of questions have on classroom activity?
4. In what directions do I want to move, based on the information provided here? How will I do so?

Class 1	Class 2	Class 3	Class 4	Class 5
Yes-No	Short Answer	Immediate Thought	Relationship	Opinion (Divergent)

RESPONSES TO STUDENT RESPONSES

Examining your responses to the responses your students make to your questions can be an enlightening learning experience. Our responses can result in unusually strong incidental learnings (see p. 86). For example, if you always answer correct student responses with "good" delivered in the same pitch and tone, the response may begin to lose the effect of positive reinforcement for which it was probably intended. It is more helpful in this case to use a wider variety of positive responses, such as "That's the same answer I had," "I agree with that answer," or "I am pleased you thought of that."

The tendency to respond to opinion answers in terms of right and wrong is also worth looking for.

Student: I think we spend too much money on the space program.

Teacher: No, the money was spent on a very worthwhile cause.

A third tendency to notice is repeating and embellishing a student's response.

Student: George Washington was the tallest president we ever had in relation to the men of his era.

Teacher: Yes, George Washington was the tallest in that sense. In actual inches Lincoln was taller, but because men were generally smaller in Washington's day, we can consider George the tallest.

By repeating and embellishing the response, the teacher leads the students to believe that the teacher must always have the last word; therefore, the student's answer will never be good enough.

Isolated cases of these responses cannot cause much of a problem, of course, but repetitive use can discourage good class discussion. There are other types of incidental learnings that your responses can create, some of them positive. For example, asking for a personal response to an opinion question such as "Why do you feel that way?" or "Are you proud of that?" can encourage the student to look more deeply into his opinions. The good questioner is aware of the types of responses that he uses most frequently and their effects. If the effects are not those he desires, he is able to change his responses to more effective ones. This activity will help you monitor your responses to student responses so that you can grasp a greater awareness of their effects and begin, if necessary, to use more positive and useful responses.

Objectives

1. To gather data about your responses to student responses.
2. To interpret the effects of your responses.
3. To choose new patterns, if necessary, for more positive effects.

Directions

METHOD ONE

Have an observer watch you teach a lesson that will involve class discussion. As he watches you teach, he fills in the accompanying worksheet by placing a mark in the box that best describes how you respond to each of your students' responses. Before class, go over the worksheet and agree on the meanings of each category, and see if you need any additions to the categories of possible responses. Use the data to answer the questions below.

METHOD TWO

Have an observer write down verbatim (or as close to verbatim as possible) your responses to your students' responses. In some cases it might be helpful to record the students' responses as well. You can also use a mechanical device, audio or video, to record the lesson. You can then analyze the data yourself, filling in the worksheet. Once you have completed the worksheet, use the data to answer the following questions.

Questions

1. Which category of response did you use most frequently? second most frequently? third?
2. Which was the least used category of response? second least used? third?
3. Which categories of response were not used at all?
4. What incidental learnings can you find for your response pattern? (Review incidental learnings on p. 86).
5. Which of your patterns do you wish to maintain?
6. Which patterns do you wish to change? What changes can you suggest?

I.   STUDENT ANSWERS CORRECTLY

teacher says "good," _____

teacher nods, _____

teacher gives no noticeable response, _____

teacher repeats answer, _____

teacher rewords answer, _____

teacher thanks student, _____

teacher praises student, _____

teacher asks student to repeat, _____

teacher looks pleased, _____

teacher adds to answer, _____

teacher uses answer to go on, _____

II.   STUDENT ANSWERS INCORRECTLY

teacher says no, asks someone else, _____

teacher says "No, try again," _____

teacher corrects student, _____

teacher leads or prods, _____

teacher ridicules student, _____

teacher encourages student, _____

III.   STUDENT RESPONDS WITH OPINION

teacher accepts answer, _____

teacher gives own answer, _____

teacher says answer is wrong, _____

teacher carries answer further, _____

teacher changes subject, _____

teacher challenges student to prove himself, _____

teacher ignores answer, _____

Follow-up

Once you have a list of possible changes in your response pattern, try to incorporate them into your next class discussion. If you are comfortable with your suggestions for change, try to make them a regular part of your questioning practices. At a later time repeat this activity to find out if in fact you have really changed in the way you planned, and if there are new response patterns for you to work on.

OPEN-ENDED STUDENT FEEDBACK

Your students can supply you with a wealth of data about your teaching. This assertion is understood by nearly every teacher. To a large extent, most teachers use students in collecting feedback in a number of ways. Tests, for example, give the teacher an indication of how well he has conveyed a given amount of material. The looks of boredom or excitement on the faces of students are another form of student feedback. Many written evaluation forms have been developed to collect student feedback, some of which help determine rehiring and pay-raise policies at the high-school and college level. These forms quantify scores relating to various aspects of teaching performance as perceived by the students.

While all types of feedback, such as those mentioned above, are useful, some types of feedback are more useful than others. We have found that systematic feedback is more useful than random feedback. Random feedback, as exemplified by the looks on students' faces, is very helpful and cannot be ignored, but it must be supplemented because it is often very difficult to make valid assumptions from such data. Moreover, it is difficult for you to initiate action to generate this kind of data when you want it.

We have also found open-ended feedback to be more useful than quantitative types. Open-ended questions give students a chance to be flexible and creative by encouraging them to express their feelings, concerns, and ideas. Although open-ended feedback poses some problems in interpretation, numerical scores may often have little meaning. Consider the following example:

1. Do you enjoy this class? Yes 65%   No 35%

The percentages offer little insight into the feelings of the students or into which aspects of the class the students enjoy or do not enjoy. A better question might be "What do you enjoy about this class? What changes would you suggest?"

The great benefit of open-ended feedback is that it helps you develop empathetic understanding for your students and gain insights into how they experience and perceive your class. Interpretation of open-ended feedback comes from open, nondefensive reception and examination of the data that you collect. Many of the activities in this book can be used to provide open-ended feedback by giving the worksheets to your students. The activities that can be used in this way are listed at the end of this particular section. The following are ten different open-ended feedback forms that are specifically designed to give you valuable and interesting data. Use them as they are or modify them to better meet your needs. Younger children can usually respond to them with only slight modifications in language.

In addition to the accompanying ten forms, the following activities may be adapted for use to gain student feedback.

There and Then, p. 24.

Values in the Classroom, p. 27.

Twenty Things You Did, p. 34.

School of the Future, p. 68.

Reaction Sheets, p. 106.

Perception Collage, p. 123.

Observation: Student Point of View, p. 126.

School Paradoxes, p. 129.

Classroom Arrangement, p. 132.

Rituals, p. 142.

Identifying Feelings, p. 152.

Teacher Walking Map, p. 175.

Student Feedback Form #1

[*Your name*] makes me feel _____ when he/she _____
_____

Because: (please be honest)

Student Feedback Form #2   **Name:**
**(for the beginning of a lesson,
activity, or unit)**

On [Subject, lesson, or activity—for example, Rockets, Shakespeare, Reading]. Please answer the following questions about the above subject accurately and honestly.

1. This subject interests me because—

2. This subject does not interest me because—

3. I would like to learn more about this subject because—

4. I am excited about studying (doing) this subject because—

5. I have apprehensions about studying (doing) this subject because—

6. I do best in this area—

7. I do worst in this area—

Student Feedback Form #3   **Name:**
(to end a lesson, activity, or
unit)

Please answer the following questions about the [lesson, activity, unit]
_____ we just completed.

1. The most significant aspects of this unit for me were—

2. The least significant aspects of this unit for me were—

3. I was most interested in—

4. I was least interested in—

5. What I would like to do again is—

6. What I would not like to do again is—

7. What I learned that I never knew before was—

8. I relearned that—

9. If I were teaching this unit, I would—

Student Feedback Form #4

Draw a picture of a good teacher. Include anything significant that you feel makes a good teacher. List any characteristics that a good teacher has.

Draw a picture of a poor teacher. Include anything significant that you feel makes a poor teacher. List any characteristics that a poor teacher has.

Student Feedback Form #5

Design an ideal lesson in [teacher or student chooses subject]. Include the following:

1. Classroom activities

2. Home activities

3. Readings

4. Teacher's role

5. Alone or in groups (if in groups, each member's task)

6. Evaluation of lesson

7. End results

8. Whatever else you choose

Student Feedback Form #6

Please mark the appropriate space on the following continua. The atmosphere in this classroom for me is—

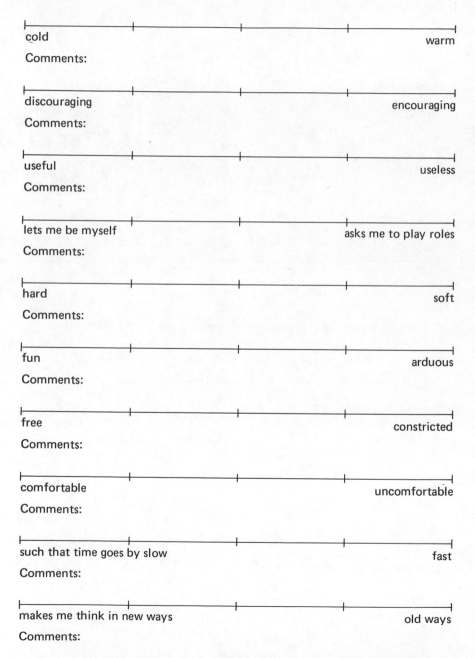

cold   warm

Comments:

discouraging   encouraging

Comments:

useful   useless

Comments:

lets me be myself   asks me to play roles

Comments:

hard   soft

Comments:

fun   arduous

Comments:

free   constricted

Comments:

comfortable   uncomfortable

Comments:

such that time goes by slow   fast

Comments:

makes me think in new ways   old ways

Comments:

Student Feedback Form #7

About students from students (to be given either altogether or separately).

1. If you were to be assigned a [class] project, name three members of the class you would like to work with.
   (1).

   (2).

   (3).

2. If you needed help in [teacher fills in subject] which three members of this class might you ask?
   (1).

   (2).

   (3).

3. If you were given a chance to interview two students in this class, whom would you choose? Why?
   (1).

   (2).

4. If you had to plan a school referendum for student rights, which three students would you want on your committee?
   (1).

   (2).

   (3).

Student Feedback Form #8

[<u>Teacher's name</u>] makes me [<u>fill in any of the feelings below</u>] when he/she...

1.

2.

3.

4.

5.

6.

7.

8.

9.

10.

11.

12.

1.	happy	7.	nervous
2.	proud	8.	impatient
3.	ashamed	9.	excited
4.	enthusiastic	10.	uncomfortable
5.	bored	11.	useful
6.	interested	12.	capable

Student Feedback Form #9   Name:

How well do you know your teacher? Please answer the following questions about him/her.

1. Favorite expression:

2. What he says when he makes a mistake:

3. What kind of car he drives:

4. Favorite song(s):

5. Hobbies:

6. Favorite clothes:

7. Where teacher went to college:

8. Where teacher stands most often in class:

9. Political beliefs:

10. Favorite sports:

11. Buys lunch or brings lunch:

12. Knows a lot about:

13. Knows little about:

14. One television show teacher watches:

15. The town teacher lives in:

16. One thing you both have in common:

17. One thing different about you two:

18. One thing teacher wants you to do:

19. One thing you can do in class to please teacher:

20. One thing you can do in class to displease teacher:

Student Feedback Form #10 (Teacher Uniqueness)

In what ways is your teacher like other teachers you have had?
1.

2.

3.

4.

5.

In what ways is your teacher unlike any teacher you have had?
1.

2.

3.

4.

5.

In what ways is your teacher like you?
1.

2.

3.

4.

5.

In what ways is your teacher unlike you?
1.

2.

3.

4.

5.

4

Log Conversations:

Comments

Barbara: We've covered so many things, Rick—data collection and interpretation, pattern identification, choosing alternatives, recycling the alternatives all over again. I think that our readers must have learned a lot about themselves if they worked on the activities seriously.

Rick: It's been an exciting project, but how could it have been anything else? We covered the integration of emotional, intellectual, and behavioral learning. We considered how a teacher develops a unique style of teaching. We looked at the ways self-knowledge really does expand one's choice of responses in the classroom. I consider those the basic issues for any teacher.

Barbara: Do you have an example at your fingertips of an instance where your self-knowledge helped you as a teacher?

Rick: I do, yes. At one time I designed and taught a course based on the activities in this book. I found myself scrutinizing very carefully what happened in that course. I discovered that it was impossible to preplan class activities because I just couldn't determine the needs of the students in advance. At the same time, I was uncomfortable with coming to class unprepared. Finally I resolved this dilemma in what I considered a creative manner that reflected the openness and responsibility that comes with knowing your teaching self. I came to class prepared with a number of options that I offered the students. I also encouraged suggestions from them. Eventually the class as a whole adopted an agenda. I suppose that if I had not understood my teaching self, I might have felt compelled to overlook the needs of the class and to use a plan anyway. That was the way teachers did it when I was a student.

Barbara: Do you have anything else you want to say, now that we're finished with this project?

Rick: Yes, I do. I found that after going through many activities, I began to internalize them. They have now become an integral part of my teaching. I find that getting feedback about my teaching and my interaction with my students is as important as any other aspect of teaching. What have you discovered?

Barbara: As I continually rediscover, change is an arduous process. I always find it difficult to actually participate in the process wholeheartedly. It's easy for me to simply read and agree. It's more difficult to spend the time and energy necessary for real self-awareness and self-direction. But the energy, when I expend it, always proves fruitful. I now use many of these activities repeatedly, and I find the changes I'm making to be highly rewarding.

Rick: I've felt that many times. One thing that helps me overcome my tendency to lethargy is working closely with others who support me and are working on themselves, too. The care and the sharing and the creative energy that comes from working with partners in learning nourish and energize me.

Barbara: That's important. I hope our readers will experience the nourishment and sense of growth that we have.

BIBLIOGRAPHY

Allport, Gordon W. *Becoming.* New Haven, Connecticut: Yale University Press, 1955.

Ashton-Warner, Sylvia. *Teacher.* New York: Simon and Schuster, 1963.

Association for Supervision and Curriculum Development. *Perceiving, Behaving, Becoming: A New Focus for Education.* Washington, D.C.: ASCD, 1962.

Berman, Louise. *New Priorities in the Curriculum.* Columbus, Ohio: Charles E. Merrill, 1968.

Borton, Terry. *Reach, Touch, and Teach: Student Concerns and Process Education.* New York: McGraw-Hill, 1970.

Brown, George. *Human Teaching for Human Learning: An Introduction to Confluent Education.* New York: Random House, 1971.

Combs, Arthur W. *The Professional Education of Teachers: A Perceptual View of Teacher Education.* Boston, Massachusetts: Allyn & Bacon, 1965.

Combs, Arthur W., Donald L. Avila, and William W. Purkey. *Helping Relationships: Basic Concepts for the Helping Professions.* Boston: Allyn & Bacon, 1971.

Curwin, G., and R. Curwin, R. Kramer, M. Simmons, K. Walsh. *Search for Values.* Dayton, Ohio: Pflaum/Standard, 1972.

Dewey, John. *Democracy and Education: An Introduction to the Philosophy of Education.* New York: Macmillan, 1916.

Dewey, John. *Experience and Education.* New York: Macmillan, 1938.

Fantini, Mario D., and Gerald Weinstein. *Making Urban Schools Work: Social Realities and the Urban School.* New York: Holt, Rinehart & Winston, 1968.

Freire, Paulo. *Pedagogy of the Oppressed,* trans. Myra B. Ramos. New York: Herder and Herder, 1968.

Fuhrmann, Steven D. and Barbara S. "Choosing, Prizing, Living by Your Values," *DPI Dispatch.* Des Moines, Iowa: Iowa State Department of Public Instruction, Vol. 1, Issue 4, February 1972, 4–5.

Glasser, William. *Schools Without Failure.* New York: Harper & Row, 1969.

Goble, Frank. *The Third Force: The Psychology of Abraham Maslow.* New York: Grossman, 1970.

Goldhammer, Robert. *Clinical Supervision: Special Methods for the Supervision of Teachers.* New York: Holt, Rinehart & Winston, 1969.

Goodman, Paul. *Growing Up Absurd.* New York: Random House, 1960.

Goodman, Paul. *The Community of Scholars.* New York: Random House, 1962.

Goodman, Paul. *Utopian Essays and Practical Proposals.* New York: Random House, 1962.

Goodman, Paul. *Compulsory Mis-Education.* New York: Horizon, 1964.

Goodman, Paul. *People or Personnel: Decentralizing the Mixed System.* New York: Random House, 1965.

Goodman, Paul. *Like a Conquered Province: The Moral Ambiguity of America.* New York: Random House, 1967.

Hansen, Søren and Jesper Jensen. *The Little Red Schoolbook,* trans. Berit Thornberry. London: Stage 1, 1971.

Harris, T. George. "A Conversation with Margaret Mead," *Psychology Today,* IV, No. 2. (July 1970), 58–63f.

Hawley, Robert and Isabel. *Personal Growth Activities for Classroom Use.* Amherst, Massachusetts: ERA, 1972.

Henry, Jules. *Culture Against Man.* New York: Random House, 1963.

Holt, John C. *How Children Fail.* New York: Dell, 1964.

Holt, John C. *How Children Learn.* New York: Dell, 1967.

Illich, Ivan D. *Deschooling Society.* New York: Harper & Row, 1971.

Johnson, David W. *Reaching Out: Interpersonal Effectiveness and Self-Actualization.* Englewood Cliffs, New Jersey: Prentice-Hall, 1972.

Johnson, John, and Arthur Seagull. "Form and Function of Affective Training of Teachers," *Phi Delta Kappan,* L, No. 3, 166–70.

Jones, Richard M. *Fantasy and Feeling in Education.* New York: New York University Press, 1968.

Kohlberg, Lawrence. "The Child as a Moral Philosopher," *Psychology Today,* II, No. 4 (September 1968), 24–30.

Kurtz, Paul, ed. *Moral Problems in Contemporary Society: Essays in Humanistic Ethics.* Englewood Cliffs, New Jersey: Prentice-Hall, 1969.

Lane, Homer. *Talks to Parents and Teachers.* New York: Schocken, 1928.

Leonard, George B. *Education and Ecstasy.* New York: Delacorte, 1968.

Macdonald, James B. "Helping Teachers Change," in *The Supervisor: Agent for Change in Teaching,* ed. James Rath and Robert R. Leeper. Washington, D.C.: ASCD, 1966.

Maslow, Abraham H. *Toward a Psychology of Being* (2nd ed.). New York: Van Nostrand Reinhold, 1968.

Maslow, Abraham H. *Motivation and Personality* (2nd ed.). New York: Harper & Row, 1970.

Mead, Margaret. *Culture and Commitment.* Garden City, New York: Doubleday, 1970.

Metcalf, Lawrence E., ed. *Values Education: Rationale, Strategies and Procedures.* Washington, D.C.: National Council for the Social Studies, 41st Yearbook, 1971.

Montagu, Ashley. *The Humanization of Man: Our Changing Conception of Human Nature.* Cleveland: World Publishing, 1962.

Neill, A. S. *Summerhill: A Radical Approach to Child Rearing.* New York: Hart, 1960.

Neill, A. S. *Freedom—Not License!* New York: Hart, 1966.

Oden, Thomas C. *The Intensive Group Experience: The New Pietism.* Philadelphia: Westminster, 1972.

Peterson, James A. *Counseling and Values: A Philosophical Examination.* Scranton, Pennsylvania: International Textbook, 1970.

Postman, Neil, and Charles Weingartner. *Teaching as a Subversive Activity.* New York: Delacorte, 1969.

Raths, Louis E., Merrill Harmin, and Sidney B. Simon. *Values and Teaching: Working with Values in the Classroom.* Columbus, Ohio: Charles E. Merrill, 1966.

Reimer, Everett. *School Is Dead: Alternatives in Education.* Garden City, New York: Doubleday, 1971.

Rogers, Carl R. *Freedom to Learn.* Columbus, Ohio: Charles E. Merrill, 1969.

Rogers, Carl. *Carl Rogers on Encounter Groups.* New York: Harper & Row, 1970.

Rokeach, Milton. *Beliefs, Attitudes and Values: A Theory of Organization and Change.* San Francisco: Jossey-Bass, 1968.

Rucker, W. Ray, V. Clyde Arnspiger, and Arthur J. Brodbeck. *Human Values in Education.* Dubuque, Iowa: Kendall/Hunt, 1969.

Shaftel, Fannie R. and George. *Role-Playing for Social Values: Decision-Making in the Social Studies.* Englewood Cliffs, New Jersey: Prentice-Hall, 1967.

Silberman, Charles E. *Crisis in the Classroom.* New York: Random House, 1970.

Simon, Sidney B., Leland W. Howe, and Howard Kirschenbaum. *Values Clarification: A Handbook of Practical Strategies for Teachers and Students.* New York: Hart, 1972.

Snitzer, Herb. *Living at Summerhill.* New York: Collier, 1964.

Sutich, Anthony J., and Miles A. Vich. *Readings in Humanistic Psychology.* New York: Free Press, 1969.

Weinstein, Gerald, and Mario D. Fantini, eds. *Toward Humanistic Education: A Curriculum of Affect.* New York: Praeger, 1970.

Whitehead, Alfred North. *The Aims of Education and Other Essays.* New York: Mentor, 1929.

Index